I0436578

Table of Contents

Chapter 1 – Introduction

The universe is under no obligation to make sense to you." – Neil deGrasse Tyson

We start this book with this quote from famous astrophysicist Neil deGrasse Tyson because it encapsulates the idea that understanding and navigating the complexities of the universe, much like those of personal finance and achieving financial independence, requires effort, curiosity, and a willingness to embrace what we may not initially understand. It aligns well with the concept of reaching financial escape velocity, where one ventures into the unknown realm of financial self-sufficiency.

In this book, we'll explore this analogy in depth, drawing parallels between the physics of escape velocity and personal finance. Just like a rocket's journey is carefully calculated and executed, achieving real financial independence requires a well-thought-out plan, a deep understanding of financial principles, and the courage to take calculated risks.

Achieving escape velocity in this context means you've accumulated enough wealth to cover your expenses without the need for additional active income. Understanding the physics behind escape velocity provides a solid foundation for grasping its financial counterpart. Escape velocity is the minimum speed needed for an object to break free from the gravitational attraction of a massive body, without further propulsion. This concept translates seamlessly into finance, where 'gravitational pull' can be seen as the regular expenses and financial obligations that keep us grounded.

Overview of Financial Independence

In today's fast-paced world, financial independence is more than a luxury; it's a necessity for securing a life of freedom and choice. Financial independence is often misunderstood as a state reserved for the wealthy or the frugal extremists. However, it's a universally attainable goal, achievable through smart planning, disciplined saving, and wise investing. This book, "Financial Escape Velocity," is designed to guide you through the journey of achieving financial autonomy, where your assets and savings are sufficient to cover your life's expenses, rendering active income optional rather than mandatory.

Why Achieve Financial Independence? In a world where financial uncertainty often looms large, the allure of financial independence is undeniable. It's about more than just amassing wealth; it's about gaining control over your time and choices. The concept of financial independence revolves around creating a life where your financial obligations do not dictate your daily decisions.

One of the most compelling reasons to strive for financial independence is the freedom it affords. Imagine a life where you're not tethered to a 9-to-5 job, where your decisions aren't driven by financial constraints, but by your passions and interests. This is the essence of financial independence – it's about living on your terms.

The FIRE Movement: A Path of Extremes? The FIRE movement, where the acronym stands for "Financial Independence Retire Early" has gained significant traction, advocating for extreme savings and investment strategies to achieve financial independence at a young age. Proponents of FIRE, like Mr. Money Mustache (Pete Adeney), argue for a frugal lifestyle and aggressive saving tactics. Adeney famously retired at 30 and now enjoys a life dictated by his interests, not financial needs. He says, "The point is to find a lifestyle that makes you happy and then save aggressively to fund it."

However, FIRE is not without its critics. Some argue that it promotes an unsustainable lifestyle of extreme frugality that can lead to burnout and social isolation. Critics also point out that the movement often assumes a higher-than-average income and fails to account for unforeseen circumstances like health issues.

Anecdotes abound on both sides of the argument. One early retiree, who achieved financial independence at 35, shared that the initial euphoria of retirement gave way to a sense of aimlessness. In contrast, others find deep satisfaction in the freedom to pursue hobbies, travel, and spend time with family without the constraints of a traditional job.

Financial independence is a highly personal journey and what works for one person may not work for another. It's crucial to consider your circumstances, values, and life goals when planning for financial independence. As financial advisor Suze Orman states, "The key to financial freedom is a balance between saving for the future and enjoying your money now."

Achieving financial independence doesn't necessarily mean the end of work. Instead, it's about having the choice to work on your terms. It's the freedom to choose your projects, set your hours, and work from anywhere. This redefinition of work aligns with the desires of many in the modern workforce, who seek meaning and flexibility in their careers.

Consider the story of a tech entrepreneur who, after achieving financial independence, chose to start a nonprofit. Without the pressure of earning a salary, he could focus on his passion for social change. Similarly, a former corporate lawyer used her financial independence to transition into teaching, a profession she found more fulfilling but less lucrative.

Ultimately, financial independence is about choice. It's not a prescription to stop working; rather, it's an invitation to redefine the role of work in your life. It's about breaking free from the financial constraints that limit your choices, allowing you to pursue your passions, whether they involve continuing to work, changing careers, or stepping away from the traditional workforce entirely.

As you embark on this journey, remember that financial independence is as much about the path as it is about the destination. It's a journey of understanding your values, redefining your relationship with money, and ultimately, crafting a life that aligns with your deepest aspirations.

Chapter 2 – Understanding Escape Velocity

"To confine our attention to terrestrial matters would be to limit the human spirit." – Stephen Hawking

The Analogy of Escape Velocity in Finance

Escape velocity is a concept in physics that describes the minimum speed needed for an object to break free from the gravitational pull of a celestial body, such as the Earth, without further propulsion. The formula for escape velocity (Ve) is given by:

$$V_\epsilon = \sqrt{\frac{2G\,M}{r}}$$

where:

- G is the gravitational constant: $6.674 \times 10^{-11}\, m^3\, kg^{-1}\, s^{-2}$,
- M is the mass of the celestial body (for Earth, it's approximately $5.972 \times 10^{24}\, kg$),
- r is the distance from the center of the celestial body to the object (for Earth, this would be the radius of Earth plus the object's altitude above the Earth's surface).

In simpler terms, escape velocity is the speed required to overcome the gravitational force of a planet or other body. For Earth, this velocity is about 11.2 km/s (about 40,233 km per hour or about 25,000 miles per hour). This means a rocket must travel at this speed to leave Earth's gravity without further propulsion.

Translating this concept into finance, achieving 'Financial Escape Velocity' involves accumulating enough assets and investments to generate sufficient passive income, overcoming the 'gravitational pull' of your regular expenses and financial obligations. Just as a rocket uses a significant amount of energy to reach escape velocity, individuals must put in considerable effort, through saving and investing, to reach a point where their financial resources can sustain their lifestyle indefinitely.

In financial terms, 'G' could be seen as the 'gravitational pull' of the cost of living where you live. When talking about physics, it is a constant in this universe. In our context of financial independence, it could be seen as a cost-of-living constant that depends on the country or region where you live. While moving to a different universe might not be an option, moving to a lower cost-of-living environment is certainly possible. This is why people consider relocating to a different city or country to make financial independence easier to ahieve.

The equivalent for mass, or 'M' in the equation above, can be seen as the amount needed to sustain your lifestyle and necessary expenses. You have some control over this too, as you can decide to forgo certain luxuries, but there is a minimum you should aim for, including critical expenses like medical insurance.

The radius, or 'r' in the equation above, can be seen in the financial analogy as the return you can sustainably expect from your savings, investments, and assets you own. Notice that 'r' is found in the denominator, meaning that it has an inverse relationship with the escape velocity. The higher the expected return, the easier it will be to attain financial escape velocity, all else equal. It is critical, however, to not misjudge the sustainable return you can expect over the long-term, otherwise you could find yourself in a situation where you belive you attained financial escape velocity, but in reality you are consuming some of your capital, and that is a recipe for a crash landing.

Finally, the escape velocity represents the amount of wealth needed to attain financial independence.

The journey to financial independence mirrors a rocket's ascent. Initially, there's a need for significant energy (savings and investments) to overcome the pull of regular expenses. Once escape velocity is achieved, the need for active propulsion (active income) is eliminated.

This book will delve into how one can accumulate this 'financial energy' through various methods like creating passive income streams, proper asset allocation and portfolio management, mitigating risks, and sustainable investing. The aim is to help you ultimately reach a state where your financial resources work for you, giving you the time and confidence to work on your true passions, much like a spacecraft gliding through space, unshackled from Earth's gravity.

Chapter 3 – Balancing Satisfaction and Resources

"The real measure of your wealth is how much you'd be worth if you lost all your money." – Anonymous

The concept of a utility function is central to economics and finance. It represents a mathematical formulation used to describe an individual's preference structure for different outcomes. Essentially, a utility function translates the satisfaction or value a person derives from various goods or scenarios into quantifiable terms.

In its simplest form, a utility function could be as straightforward as assigning a numerical value to the satisfaction gained from consuming a product. However, the reality is often more complex. Utility functions vary significantly from person to person, reflecting diverse preferences, risk tolerances, and life circumstances.

There are some paradoxes which we can use to prove that money in general does not have a linear utility function for humans. Let us present to you the St. Petersburg Paradox, which is one of the most famous illustrations of the complexities in utility functions. This paradox presents a game where a fair coin is tossed until it lands heads up. The payoff doubles for each tails shown, starting at $2. Mathematically, this game has an infinite expected value, suggesting that a rational person should be willing to pay any finite amount to play. Yet, in reality, most people would not pay large sums to participate.

This paradox highlights a critical aspect of utility functions: they are not always linear. The value or utility of money to an individual does not increase indefinitely with the amount. There's a diminishing marginal utility, meaning as wealth increases, the additional satisfaction gained from an extra dollar decreases. This paradox also shows that utility functions are very likely influenced by behavioral and psychological factors. People have a hard time imagining or visualizing the coin land tails down many times in a row, and are therefore unwilling to pay much to take the bet. Still, they are ready to purchase a lottery ticket, where they also have an incredibly small probability of making a lot of money, and which typically offers a negative expected return. Most people know that, on average, participants lose money in lotteries. However, millions of people willingly buy lottery tickets. This behavior can partly be explained by the non-linear nature of utility functions. For many, the small chance of winning a life-changing amount of money has a high utility, outweighing the utility of keeping a relatively insignificant amount of money. At the same time, they are probably thinking a lot less about probabilities, and are not forced to visualize a coin landing time after time tails down, as is the case with the St. Petersburg Paradox. This tells us that people have non-linear utility functions, and they are significantly influenced by psychological factors.

Research in behavioral economics, such as the work of Daniel Kahneman and Amos Tversky, investigates this type of behaviour further. For example, their Prospect Theory suggests that people evaluate potential losses and gains differently, with losses often having a more significant impact than similarly sized gains. This asymmetry also helps explain why people are willing to participate in lotteries, despite the negative expected return. The fact that pain of losing money is often more intense than the pleasure of gaining the same amount, causes loss aversion. This asymmetry has significant implications for both individuals and businesses, influencing risk tolerance and decision-making.

In personal finance, acknowledging the non-linearity of utility functions is crucial. It explains why individuals make certain financial decisions that might seem irrational at face value. For instance, some might choose to spend on luxury items or experiences, not just for the inherent value of the product or service but for the satisfaction or status they derive from it.

However, this non-linear nature of utility also leads to counterintuitive implications. For instance, the same amount of money can have vastly different utilities for different people or even for the same person under different circumstances. This variability makes personal financial planning uniquely challenging, as it must account for individual preferences and the diminishing marginal utility of wealth.

Further complicating things, the value of assets and even money can change over time. There are surprising instances where the value of money can drop to close to zero or, even become negative. For example, in hyperinflation scenarios, like those experienced in post-World War I Germany or more recently in Zimbabwe, the value of money plummeted so drastically that people found more value in using currency notes for purposes other than transactions, such as wallpaper or fashion items. In these cases, the sheer abundance and devaluation of money rendered it practically useless for its intended purpose.

A surprising scenario where the value of money can even turn negative is when tax schemes are not well designed. For instance, there have been situations where an employee found out that a small salary increase resulted in less net pay, all because she is now in a higher tax bracket. The net present value of money can also change as a function of interest rates. For example, some European countries and Japan have at times experienced negative interest rates. Here, depositing money in banks or buying certain bonds meant the holder would incur a cost, a situation that turns the conventional understanding of money's value on its head. This has multiple consequences, from changing the utility function of money, to decreasing its usefulness as fuel for our financial independence rocket. We need to build a solid rocket, one that can work even with negative interest rates!

There is also a point beyond which additional money ceases to add significant value or utility. This concept is illustrated by the law of diminishing marginal utility in economics. Once basic needs are met, each additional dollar yields less and less utility. For ultra-high-net-worth individuals, the marginal utility of additional wealth becomes almost negligible. Their fifth luxury or sports car is probably not going to change their overall happiness very much.

Why are we spending so much time talking about economic utility functions and marginal returns on wealth? We believe most people would maximize their life's happiness if they reduced the time it took them to reach financial escape velocity, even if it meant lower terminal wealth. Going back to the rocket analogy, they are spending too many years filling their rockets with fuel, multiples of the fuel they need to reach escape velocity assuming a reasonable lifestyle. Sometimes they come to this realization in old age, when they have become billionaires, but with few years left to enjoy life. An extreme example can be found in Venus, Steve Jobs' superyatch, which unfortunately he never got to use despite spending more than one hundred million dollars on it. This has not stopped other billionaires from spending even more on their own superyatchs, with some exceeding the billion dollars mark. These are expensive assets that usually cost significant amounts to maintain, usually generating negative cash flows to their owners. These are example of the types of assets you want to avoid, as they slow you down, instead of providing acceleration to quickly reach financial escape velocity. Even for the wealthiest individuals, the ability to meaningfully spend or invest vast fortunes is limited by the scale of available opportunities. Money's utility, in this sense, is capped not just by personal thresholds but also by the economic context in which it exists.

The non-linear utility function of money reveals a complex relationship between financial decisions and outcomes. It challenges the traditional notion of money as a straightforward, quantifiable entity and underscores the nuanced role it plays in our lives. Understanding this non-linearity is crucial for effective personal and business financial decision-making, highlighting the need for a sophisticated, nuanced approach to financial planning and strategy. Recognizing this can lead to more effective financial decision-making, as it considers not just the financial value, but also the satisfaction from different financial choices. In the end, the utility function underscores a fundamental truth in personal finance: money's value is not just in its quantity, but in its ability to fulfill individual preferences, needs, and aspirations.

Chapter 4: Risk

"Risk comes from not knowing what you're doing." – Warren Buffett

In finance, risk is an ever-present invisible force, subtly influencing every decision and outcome. We can visualize it as uncertainty in each of the variables in the escape velocity formula. For example, there is risks in not obtaining the expected returns from our assets. There is risk that we might need more money to maintain the type of lifestyle we are aiming for, or that we might need money for an emergency. There is risk that cost-of-living could increase more than expected where we live, or even globally. Understanding risk is therefore crucial for anyone aiming to achieve financial escape velocity, and it usually comes in three different forms.

1. Known Knowns: These are risks we are aware of and understand. An example would be the interest rate risk for bond investments, where the risk is quantifiable and often predictable.

2. Known Unknowns: These risks are recognized but their impacts are uncertain. Stock market volatility is a classic example. While investors know markets can be volatile, predicting the magnitude and timing of market movements is challenging.

3. Unknown Unknowns: Perhaps the most daunting, these risks are unforeseeable and impossible to plan for. The Covid pandemic, for instance, was largely an unknown unknown, catching many investors and experts by surprise, and resulting in general changes in behaviour that would have been almost impossible to predict. For example, we do not think many office real estate investors were paying much attention to the possibility of a step change in the percentage of people working from home.

Beyond these categories, financial risks can be further classified into market risk, credit risk, liquidity risk, operational risk, and systemic risk, each with its unique characteristics and implications.

Traditionally, financial risk assessment has often relied on the Gaussian, or bell curve, which assumes a normal distribution of outcomes. However, this approach underestimates the likelihood of extreme events. In reality, financial markets exhibit 'fat tails' — extreme positive and negative outcomes occur more frequently than a normal distribution would predict. Most significant risks in finance often lie in the tails of the distribution, where rare but impactful events reside. The difficulty in predicting these extreme market events lies in their rarity and the complex interplay of factors that lead to them. The Global Financial Crisis of 2008, for instance, was a result of a complex mix of high-risk mortgage lending, excessive borrowing, and failure of financial regulations. On the positive side, the unprecedented rise of companies like Amazon and Google defied traditional market predictions, creating enormous wealth for early investors.

We do not want a negative tail risk to derail our financial rocket, which is why we have to be careful to protect against unforseen challenges. This is why things like having good medical coverage and property insurance are so important, and why having an emergency cash fund usually makes sense even if it delivers low financial returns. An emergency fund helps reduce the risk that you might be forced to sell stocks or real estate at an inopportune time, and it brings optionality to take advantage of positive risk. Positive risk can come in the form of an unexpected investment opportunity. A great example of this was the 1987 stock market crash, where the sudden collapse of the market gave people with immediate liquidity the opportunity to purchase shares in companies at deeply discounted prices.

Managing financial risk is threfore a balancing act between caution and opportunity. Diversification is the first line of defense — spreading investments across various asset classes can mitigate the impact of a downturn in any single market. Another strategy is hedging, which involves taking offsetting positions in different investments to reduce the risk of adverse price movements. While effective, hedging can be complex and costly. Investment risk can also be managed through insurance products, like options and futures, which provide a safety net against market downturns. However, these instruments can be complex and might introduce additional risks. Each risk management strategy has its advantages and disadvantages. Diversification is simple and effective but might limit the potential for high returns. Hedging offers precise risk control but can be expensive and complex. We believe for most people a combination of having some cash, a well desgined investment portfolio, and insuring against unforseen expenses, is probably the best approach to mitigate risk. We will talk a lot more about asset classes and porfolio allocation in a future chapter.

A key aspect of risk management is understanding one's risk tolerance. This involves an honest assessment of how much risk one is willing and able to take on. It's also important to recognize that not all risks can be eliminated; some must be accepted for the potential of higher returns. Still, we must evaluate which risks can slow us down enough to derail financial escape velocity, and which risks we can afford to ignore. For example, a successful startup entrepreneur might have reached enough wealth to surpass financial escape velocity, to a point where an unforseen large medical bill or property damage would not derail it. In such a case, the much bigger risk would be not selling some of the shares and buying other investments.

Risk, the invisible force in finance, demands respect and understanding. By recognizing the various types of risks, acknowledging the limitations of traditional risk models, and employing a thoughtful mix of risk management strategies, investors can navigate the financial universe more safely. The key is not to avoid risk altogether but to manage it in a way that aligns with one's financial goals and risk tolerance. This balance is crucial for achieving long-term financial stability and reaching one's financial escape velocity.

Chapter 5: What's Your Number?

"It is in the selection of what is necessary, and the leaving behind of what is comfortable, that one finds the balance for a journey. Pack too light, and you're unprepared; too heavy, and you're overwhelmed."
– Ed Stafford

The Quest for the Magic Number

In the world of high-stakes consulting and finance, "the number" has become a semi-serious, semi-jocular topic of conversation. It's that elusive figure, supposedly enough to let one comfortably exit the rat race. There's an anecdote about a consultant who, when asked about his number, replied, "It keeps changing; the closer I get, the further it seems." Meanwhile, a finance executive once admitted, "It's not just about the amount. It's about what it represents - freedom, choices, and no more Monday blues."

Identifying this number is critical in personal finance. It turns abstract concepts like 'saving for retirement' into a concrete goal. For instance, if your freedom number is $2 million, every financial decision can be weighed against how it helps or hinders reaching this goal. As the chapter introduction quote suggests, the need for careful balance and thoughtful decision-making are key when planning for financial independence.

The first important thing to understand about this number is that it is a net number, where you evaluate your current financial status, or total rocket fuel, by adding your assets and substracting your liabilities. For example, if you have $500,000 in savings and investments but $200,000 in debt, your net starting point is $300,000. It is often a good idea to give high priority to debt repayment, as it usually carries a high interest rate that is higher than what you can expect your assets to generate in a convervative scenario. However, this is not always the case, and sometimes it is preferrable to simply service the debt and invest any excess income.

One common example is when people are able to lock-in a great mortgage rate on a property. When the Federal Reserve reduced interest rates to close to zero, some people were able to negotiate fixed-rate mortgages with durations of 30 years, at a less than a 3% interest rate.[1]

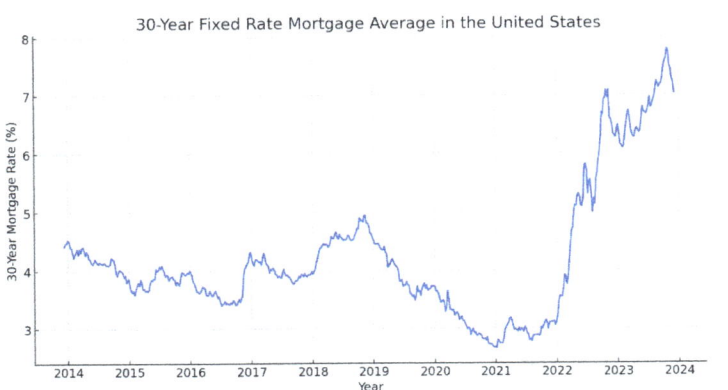

Clearly, if you were one of the lucky people that was able to get financing at such a low rate you will likely be better off putting excess savings into other investments rather than paying your mortgage early. By the way, deciding when to take action, such as deciding when to refinance your mortgage or purchase a home, can be aided by the scientific findings of a field called "optimal stopping". We'll talk more about it in a future chapter.

For now, what is important to retain is that your financial escape velocity is a net worth number, that takes into account assets and debts, and which we can estimate. It starts with your total annual cost of living, including any necessary insurance and medical costs, as well as a budget for leisure activities like travel. It will vary greatly by lifestyle choices, and the place in the world you plan to live in. If you are aiming for a globe-trotting retirement, it might require a larger number than a modest, home-centered lifestyle. Especially if you already own your home. However, if you plan to relocalte to a place where cost of living is significantly cheaper, and plan to permanently live there, it can actually make your financial escape velocity number much smaller. Of course, make sure you follow the proper immigration requirements of the place where you want to relocate to, and do as much research as you possibly can about living there before making the move. If you decide to move, try to sell or donate things you will no longer need, as self-storage is expensive.

1Freddie Mac, 30-Year Fixed Rate Mortgage Average in the United States [MORTGAGE30US], retrieved from FRED, Federal Reserve Bank of St. Louis; https://fred.stlouisfed.org/series/MORTGAGE30US, December 10, 2023.

Once you know the cost-of-living of the place, or places, where you plan to live, and the lifestyle you would like to have, you basically have the 'G' and the 'M' for the escape velocity formula. This will allow you to create an annual budget that includes all your expenses and planned activities. Let's imagine you calculate you can live with a $35,000 annual budget where you plan to live. Now all we need is to estimate a reasonable rate of return to determine the 'fuel' we need. Given that inflation can erode the value of money over time, it is important to use a real rate of return (that is after inflation). For example, an investment might have a nominal yield of 9%, but if inflation is 5%, the real return is 4%. Historically, a well designed investment portfolio made up of stocks and bonds has been able to exceed that threshold. In fact, financial planners usually refer to it as the "4% rule", as they believe their clients should not withdraw annually more than 4% of the value of their accounts. With the 4% rule you need 25 times your annual budget to achieve financial escape velocity. For example, for some with a total $35,000 annual budget the 4% rule would require reaching a net worth of $875,000. We believe the 4% rule is a good starting point, but we believe savy investors can aim for more aggressive real rates of return. Significantly increasing the allocation to other asset classes, such as stocks and real estate, and reducing that of bonds, can make a 7-8% real return realistic, though certainly not guaranteed. At the same time, investors that want to be extremely cautiaus might want to only consider Treasury bonds. We are writing this book at the end of 2023, currently the real rate of return for 10 year Treasury bonds is close to 2%. That means multiplying by 50 your annual budget, requiring $1.75 million for someone with the same $35,000 annual budget.

In future chapters we'll talk about strategies that can help an investor get closer to a 7% to 8% real rate of return, including things like trying to avoid selling shares after a market crash, looking for opportunities in international markets, and consiering other asset classes such as real estate and infrastructure funds. We'll also run some Monte Carlo simulations to evaluate results assuming various market scenarios and the resulting range of outcomes.

Chapter 6: Asset Allocation Optimization

"Do not put all your eggs in one basket." – Warren Buffett

Asset allocation is akin to crafting a sophisticated financial rocket; it's about assembling the right combination of elements to propel you towards your financial goals while managing the risks of the journey. Just as a rocket engineer optimizes various components, fuel type like liquid hydrogen, and oxidyzer like nitrogen or liquid oxygen, for a successful launch and flight, an investor must balance different asset classes, allocations, and rebalancing techniques to optimize for returns and risk.

The Markowitz Portfolio Model

The Markowitz Portfolio Model, which is basically the base for Modern Portfolio Theory (MPT), was introduced by Harry Markowitz in 1952, revolutionizing the world of finance. The theory is also known as the Markowitz Mean Variance Model. The model suggests that it's not enough to look at the expected risk and return of one particular stock. By investing in more than one stock, an investor can reap the benefits of diversification – chief among them, a reduction in the riskiness of the portfolio.

MPT is grounded in the idea of an 'efficient frontier' – a set of optimal portfolios offering the maximum possible expected return for a given level of risk. It employs standard deviation of portfolio returns as a measure of risk and suggests that any rational investor will choose a portfolio from the efficient frontier, as these portfolios are expected to yield the highest returns for a given level of risk.

Criticisms and Shortcomings

Despite its foundational status in finance, the Markowitz Portfolio Model is not without criticism. Many argue that it relies heavily on historical data to predict future returns, which can make it extremely unreliable. The model also assumes that all investors are rational and markets are efficient, which behavioral economists argue does not hold true in the real world. Additionally, it does not account for the impact of external economic events that can drastically affect market conditions.

A Better Alternative

The Kelly criterion, developed by John L. Kelly Jr. in 1956, has emerged as a sophisticated and potentially superior approach to portfolio optimization. This criterion focuses on maximizing the expected logarithm of wealth, which is equivalent to maximizing the expected geometric growth rate of an investment portfolio. The key advantage of the Kelly criterion is its ability to balance the trade-off between risk and return in a way that maximizes long-term wealth.

One of the primary reasons the Kelly criterion is considered superior for certain investors is its emphasis on capital preservation while still capitalizing on growth opportunities. Unlike traditional methods, which may prioritize short-term gains or overly conservative approaches, the Kelly criterion provides a calculated strategy to optimize bet size and allocation in a way that maximizes long-term growth potential.

However, the Kelly criterion can be aggressive, often suggesting a high degree of leverage, which may not be suitable for all investors, especially those with lower risk tolerances or shorter investment horizons. To address this, many investors and portfolio managers use a fractional Kelly approach, which involves investing a fraction of the amount suggested by the full Kelly criterion. This approach reduces potential volatility and drawdowns while still leveraging the core benefits of the Kelly framework.

One of the key advantages of the Kelly criterion investing model is that it maximizes long-run wealth, and minimizes the expected time to reach large financial goals. In other words, in the long-run it has been mathematically proven to beat every other strategy, and to provide the best allocation to minimize the expected amount of time needed to reach a certain financial target (e.g. doubling or tripling your capital).

To be able to use the Kelly criterion approach to portfolio optimization you need to be able to estimate the return probability distribution of an investment. This can be extremely hard to do accurately, especially for stocks, as there is significant uncertainty to the average expected return, and even the geometrical form of the probability distribution of returns. In many cases it can look like a Guassian, or normal, curve, usually with fatter tails, but in other cases it can even have more than one peak, resulting in a bimodal or multimodal distribution. The end result is that these estimation uncertainties can result in allocations that are not optimal. According to the Kelly criterion investing approach, betting a higher percentage than the one recommended by the framework results in lower expected returns. Due to uncertainties, an investor can be left "over-betting", which increases risks while reducing expected returns. For these reasons, investors often bet a fraction of what the Kelly criterion approach recommends, for example, half-Kelly means investing half the optimal percentage of the portfolio. Many successful investors are believed to follow to a certain degree this approach, including Warren Buffett and Bill Gross. This is deduced by their investment sizing decisions, putting significant portions of their portfolios in their highest conviction investments. Buffett currently has more than 41% of its stock portfolio invested in Apple, and about 68% in his top four investments.[2] This is probably too much concentration for most investors, and a good rule of thumb is to never put more than 20% in one stock, even if it is a very solid and stable business. Research has shown that after about 30 different companies, diversification tends to add very little benefit. What is more important is to have different industry and sector exposures, as having 50 technology stocks might prove more risky than having a portfolio of 20 stocks coming from six or seven different sectors. The key idea to retain from the Kelly criterion approach to portfolio optimization is that you should not shy from significantly over-weighting your highest conviction investment ideas, as long as you understand the company and its risks very well. In some cases this could mean putting 5% of the portfolio in the top idea, in other cases it could mean putting 20%. The key idea is well summarized by Charlie T. Munger, Buffett's long-time

2   https://www.nasdaq.com/articles/68-of-warren-buffetts-$334-billion-portfolio-is-invested-in-only-4-stocks

business partner who used to advice that good investment ideas are rare, when the odds are greatly in your favour you should allocate heavily.

If you want to be more precise, you can model every investment with a return probability distribution curve, the run a Monte Carlo simulation giving different weights to the each option. You should run each allocation multiple times to estimate the mean value of the logarithm of the resulting wealth. This will give you an idea of the expected logarithm of resulting wealth for that portfolio allocation, and the optimal allocation will be the one the maximizes it. The formula for maximizing the expected logarithm of wealth is shown below, where W is the total wealth resulting the simulation of a given allocation.

$$max \, E \left[\log(W) \right]$$

Interestingly, to an individual with logarithmic utility the Kelly bet maximizes expected utility. While different persons will have different utility functions, logarithmic utility is a very reasonable approximation. After all, as we discussed previously, having ten times more money usually does not translate into being ten times happier. Investors that have made fortunes using this allocation strategy include Edward O. Thorp and Jim Simons, together with other strategies that have them a valuable edge. A few books worth reading to learn more about these investors and the Kelly Criterion include: Kelly Capital Growth Investment Criterion; Fortune's Formula: The Untold Story Of The Scientific Betting System That Beat The Casinos And Wall Street; A Man For All Markets: From Las Vegas To Wall Street, How I Beat The Dealer And The Market; The Man Who Solved The Market: How Jim Simons Launched The Quant Revolution.

Chapter 7: Asset Types

"Diversification is a protection against ignorance." – Warren Buffett

In the journey of financial planning and investment, different asset types serve as the fuel, propelling investors towards their goals. Each asset class comes with its own set of characteristics, risks, and potential returns. Understanding these is crucial for crafting a well-diversified and balanced portfolio.

Still, we believe most investors need exposure to just three or four of these asset classes, and in many cases the more complex asset classes can be avoided if the investor does not have enough knowledge about them. For example, investing in startups can be extremely profitable, but most startups end up failing. Even investing in venture capital funds can be too risky, as most of them have underperformed the market over long periods of time when measuring their performance after fees. There have been some extremely successful VC funds, but the vast majority has failed to outperfom the S&P 500 index, once their hefy fees are taken into account. Similarly, some private equity and distressed credit funds have delivered extraordinary returns, but they can be difficult to access and often have high minimum investment requirements, as well as high fees. Even some insitutional investors with access to sought after VC funds appear disappointed. This analysis shared in a Harvard Business Review article is a little dated, but still very relevant.[3]

> We analyzed the Kauffman Foundation's experience investing in nearly 100 VC funds over 20 years. We found that only 20 of our funds outperformed the markets by the 3% to 5% annually that we expect to compensate us for the fees and illiquidity we incur by investing in private rather than public equity. Even worse, 62 of our 100 funds failed to beat the returns available from a small-cap public index.

We believe that for the vast majority of people, a combination of cash investments, US and international equities, private and public real estate, and governement and corporate bonds are enough to build a solid investment portfolio. This can be complemented with other revenue streams that help create passive income, such as a blog or newsletter, an e-commerce business, or royalties from writing a book. With that in mind, let's explore the main asset classes in more detail, and the roles they play in an investment strategy.

1. Stocks (Public Equities)

Stocks represent ownership in a company. They are known for their potential for high returns, but they also come with higher risk, especially in the short term. Within stocks, there are various categories like large-cap, mid-cap, and small-cap stocks, each offering different risk-return profiles. Billionaire investor Warren Buffett, is a strong proponent of investing in stocks, particularly in companies with strong fundamentals and long-term growth potential. He sees stocks as a partial interest in a great business, and while his preference is to buy complete businesses when possible, he is happy purchasing a slice of a great business in the public

---

3   https://hbr.org/2013/05/six-myths-about-venture-capitalists

markets. Some of his best investments have been in public companies, where normal investors could have bought the shares at the same price he paid for them.

One of the most common mistakes people make with stocks is trading to frequently. If you buy shares in a company, the performance you obtain will tend to approximate the performance of the business. For example, if you invest in a company that grows revenue and profits at 15% for two decades, it is very likely that the share price will appreciate by close to 15% too. That is, unless you underpaid or overpaid by an extreme amount. Outside of bubbles and panics, most shares tend to be relatively reasonably valued, and you can expect results similar to the business performance if you wait long enough. Charlie T. Munger, Buffett's business partner liked to say that *"The big money is not in the buying and the selling, but in the waiting."* Munger's quote emphasizes the importance of patience in investing, particularly when it comes to holding onto high-quality investments. It suggests that the most significant returns are often realized by those who identify exceptional companies and then hold onto these investments over a long period, allowing their value to compound. This means that investors should be looking for and investing heavily in special, high-quality companies, and then patiently waiting for these investments to yield substantial returns.

So how can we identify this special type of company? One of the secrets is figuring out if a company has a competitive moat, or a special type of advantage that protect it from its competitors.

Understanding the Importance of Business Moats

The concept of a 'business moat' is central to identifying companies that possess a sustainable competitive advantage. This term, popularized by Warren Buffett, refers to a company's ability to maintain competitive advantages over its rivals in order to protect its long-term profits and market share. Buffett has famously said that *"It's far better to buy a wonderful company at a fair price than a fair company at a wonderful price."*
Let's explore the different sources of competitive advantage that contribute to a business moat.

Cost/Scale Advantage
Companies that achieve cost advantages typically produce goods or services at a lower cost compared to their competitors, often due to economies of scale, more efficient production techniques, or unique access to low-cost materials. This advantage allows them to undercut competitors on price or achieve higher profit margins. Walmart and Costco are prime examples, leveraging their massive scale to offer lower prices that competitors find hard to match.

Intellectual Property and Brands
Intellectual property (IP), such as patents, trademarks, and copyrights, can provide a strong moat. Patents protect technological innovations, giving companies like Pfizer or Intel a temporary monopoly to exploit their creations. Similarly, strong brands like Coca-Cola or Apple create customer loyalty and pricing power, which are significant competitive advantages. The strength of a brand can often lead customers to choose a familiar product over cheaper alternatives.

Network Effects

Network effects occur when a product or service becomes more valuable as more people use it. This is a powerful moat, especially in the technology sector. For instance, social media platforms like Facebook or services like Airbnb and Uber benefit immensely from network effects. The more users these platforms have, the more valuable they become to each user, creating a self-reinforcing cycle that new competitors find difficult to break.

Efficient Scale

This advantage occurs in industries where the market is effectively served by one or a few companies, and there is no benefit for new entrants to compete. It's often seen in utility companies or niche industries. For example, a small regional utility company can operate efficiently at a scale that meets the demand of its service area, deterring others from entering the market due to the high costs and limited potential for additional revenue.

Switching Costs

High switching costs create a barrier for customers to change to a competitor, thus creating a moat. This can be due to high financial costs, time constraints, or effort involved in switching. Companies like Adobe or Microsoft benefit from high switching costs, as customers who invest heavily in learning and integrating their software are less likely to switch to competing products.

The concept of a business moat, while rooted in the principles laid out by investors like Warren Buffett, has been significantly popularized by Morningstar. This investment research firm has been instrumental in bringing the concept into mainstream financial analysis. Morningstar analysts systematically evaluate companies to assign them a moat rating, which has become a key metric for investors assessing the long-term sustainability of a business's competitive advantage. When assigning a moat rating, Morningstar analysts look for specific characteristics that indicate a durable competitive advantage. These include a company's market dominance, pricing power, operational efficiency, and the ability to innovate. Financial ratios such as return on equity (ROE), return on invested capital (ROIC), and gross margin are closely scrutinized. High and consistent ROE or ROIC, for instance, can indicate a company efficiently utilizes its capital and has a strong competitive position. Apart from financial ratios, Morningstar's evaluation also considers factors like brand strength, customer loyalty, cost advantages, and the company's scale compared to its competitors. The presence of barriers to entry in the company's industry is another crucial factor. These barriers could be due to technology, regulatory hurdles, or substantial initial capital requirements, which make it challenging for new competitors to enter the market.

The strength and sustainability of a company's moat are continually assessed, as changes in market dynamics or company strategy can impact its competitive position. Morningstar's moat rating thus serves as a dynamic and insightful tool for investors looking to gauge the long-term investment potential of a company. By focusing on both qualitative and quantitative aspects, Morningstar's approach provides a comprehensive view of a company's ability to sustain its competitive advantage over time. What's more, you can use the idea of a "business moat" for your personal business, in fact Warren Buffett asks the managers in charge of their private businesses that they own completely to "focus on expanding the moat".

> *"So we think in terms of that moat and the ability to keep its width and its impossibility of being crossed as the primary criterion of a great business. And we tell our managers we want the moat widened every year. That doesn't necessarily mean the profit will be more this year than it was last year because it won't be sometimes. However, if the moat is widened every year, the business will do very well. When we see a moat that's tenuous in any way -it's just too risky. We don't know how to evaluate that. And, therefore, we leave it alone."*- Warren Buffett

If you own a small private business, establishing and protecting a competitive edge is vital. This can often be achieved through intellectual property rights, such as copyrights, trademarks, and patents. Securing these rights provides a form of a moat, safeguarding the uniqueness of their products or services. A small tech company with a patented technology, for example, can defend itself against larger competitors, maintaining its market position and profitability.

International Stocks

Investing in stocks from around the world can provide diversification benefits and broaden the opportunity set for investors. Relative valuations from country to country tend to vary, and at a given time shares in one market might offer more value compared to the US. There is no doubt that the US has many wonderful businesses, but at times it trades at a very significant premium compared to other markets. Certain sectors are dominated by international companies, for example, the luxury market is dominated by European conglomerates that have delivered outstanding returns to investors.

Emerging markets can also offer great investing opportunities sometimes, but it is important to be careful to understand the risks as well. Companies operating in emerging economies are some times less supervised with respect to their accounting and operations, increasing risks. In any case, don't be afraid to look at companies from around the world. Adding some international companies to your portfolio can provide diversification, and remember that there are wonderful companies in other countries too, and they are some times cheaper just because they are based outside the US.

Small Cap Stocks

Some people talk about small caps as a specific investment asset. These are simply stocks of smaller companies that usually offer high growth potential. However, they also present higher risk and volatility compared to large-cap stocks, and they tend to have more difficulty accessing cheap financing. Peter Lynch, a renowned mutual fund manager, was known for his focus on small-cap stocks, leveraging their growth potential to deliver substantial returns. The previous discussion about "business moats" also applies here, with the exception that sometimes they are less evident. However, if you are right, this can mean investing in a great company when it is just getting started growing. Imagine you lived in Seattle at the time

Starbucks opened its first few stores. The brand is not yet famous, but you had a wonderful experience as a customer, and realize they are quickly opening stores in more places. You could have used that information to analyze its stock and make a purchase, and a few decades later you would probably be very pleased with the returns.

The key takeaway is that you should evaluate stocks as an interest in a business, and great businesses can be found at different stages of their lifecycle, and in different regions of the world.

2. Bonds

Bonds are fixed-income instruments representing a loan made by the investor to the issuer (government or corporate). They are considered less risky than stocks and provide a fixed income stream, making them a staple in conservative portfolios.Government bonds are issued by governments and are considered very safe, typically offering lower returns, at least in developed economies. High-yielding government bonds can be found in some emerging markets, but we believe that assessing the risk of default is difficult, so we would advice most investors to stay away from them. If an investor wants a slightly higher return than what government bonds are offering in developed economies, they can look at corporate bonds. These are issued by companies, and usually offer higher returns than government bonds but carry higher risk in the form of credit risk. Credit risk simply means the risk that the company will not pay the investor the interest or capital back. For this reason it is usually a good idea for most investors to limit themselves to "investment grade" corporate bonds. These are companies that have been evaluated by a third pary ratings agency, which has determined the risk of default to be very low.

The concept of business moats is also relevant for bond investors. Companies with strong competitive moats are generally more stable and profitable, reducing the risk of default on their bond obligations. Investors in corporate bonds, therefore, benefit from evaluating the strength of a company's moat. A company with a solid moat is more likely to have steady cash flows and the ability to meet its debt obligations, making its bonds a safer investment.

3. Private and Public Real Estate (REITs)

Real estate can also be an interesting investing option for many investors, but given the high transaction costs and risks associated with purchasing a property, investors should understand the market very well and make sure the property has no serious issues. It is also critical to time the purchase well, to make sure you are getting good value for your money. We are writing this book as 2023 is coming to an end, and housing affordability is close to a 30 year low. While there will always be some interesting opportunitity to purchase a home in a certain market, in general right now it is a particularly bad time to find good deals. Potential investors can check housing affordability indices or tools to get an idea if it is a good time or not to purchase a home.[45]

4   https://edition.cnn.com/interactive/2023/06/homes/housing-market-prices-affordability-dg/
5   Why buying a house in the US is so hard right now, https://www.youtube.com/watch?v=Exza1UYxXXM

While buying a home can allow investors to create a passive income stream by renting it to someone long-term, or putting it in a short-term rental platform like AriBnb, another option can be to simply purchase shares in a public real estate investment trust (REIT), which allow investors to invest in portfolios of real estate assets. Investors have to be careful when analyzing the different REIT options available, but some have provided spectacular returns to investors. One example is Prologis, which is the global leader in industrial warehouses, another one is Alexandria Real Estate that rents Class A office properties with labs, usually clustered in urban life science and technology campuses. Since its IPO it has outperformed even Berkshire Hathaway, Buffett's investment vehicle. The advantage of public REITs is that they offer real estate exposure, the high liquidity of stock investments, and many offer attractive dividends that tend to grow over time.

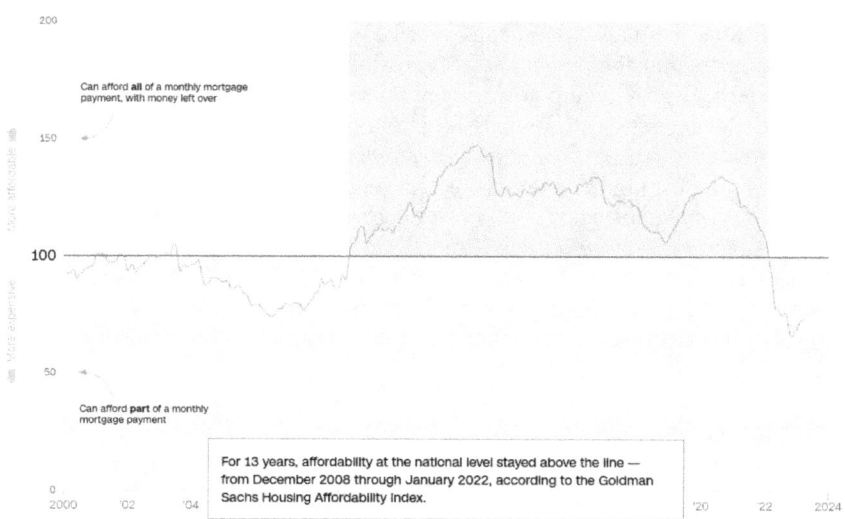

Source: CNN.com

In real estate investing, the equivalent of a business moat is often the location of the property. A prime location can act as a significant competitive advantage, affecting the property's value, rental income potential, and resilience to market fluctuations. Properties in sought-after neighborhoods, near essential amenities, or in areas with limited supply of land, tend to maintain their value and desirability over time, much like a business with a strong moat.

4. Cash investments

It is usually a good idea to have part of the investment portfolio in cash investments. This can be money maret funds, short-term certificates of deposit, etc. They typically provide a low return that is close to the rate of inflation. The real value comes from the optionality it provides. Having part of the portfolio in cash means that if the market crashes, and you have an unexpected expense, you are less likely to be forced to sell investments at a low price. It also gives you firepower to invest when these opportunities present themselves. If there are few attractive investment opportunities, it is probably a good idea to increase the allocation to cash. Coversely, you might want to have invest some of the cash available if great investment opportunities come along.

Asset Allocation Among Different Types

The famous study by Brinson, Hood, and Beebower[6] shows that asset allocation decisions account for a significant portion of portfolio returns. Diversification across these asset types can reduce risk and improve returns over the long term. The different asset types in a portfolio are like various fuel types for a journey; each serves a specific purpose and brings its own advantages and risks. A well-crafted portfolio considers the balance of these assets in alignment with the investor's goals and risk appetite. As many famous investors have noted, the key is not in picking the 'best' asset class but in how these assets are allocated and balanced to work in harmony towards achieving financial objectives. Younger investors can also take more risks as there is less uncertainty about long-term returns, and if there is a stock market or real estate crash, they can wait for things to normalize. On the other hand, older investors will want to be a little bit more cautius, and allocate more towards lower risk assets. Below we show two example allocations, one for someone in his 20's, the other for someone in their 60's.

For example, the young investor can allocate heavily towards stocks, which tend to have very high rates of return, even if they can experience higher volatility and drawdowns. The upper limit should still be around 80%, followed by some bond investments, and the rest in REITs and cash.

We can approximate the expected return using long-term historical returns for the different asset classes. It will of course depend enormously of how overvalued/undervalue each asset class is at the moment of making the investments. Still, using historical averages in the US we can have a very rough approximation. These are just estimates based on historical averages and may not accurately predict future returns.

The model portfolio for the young investor could be expected to deliver nominal annual returns of ~9%. Inflation in the US has averaged about 3% historically, which means he can probably withdraw about 6% of the portfolio value annually. This number is useful to estimate the necessary amount of "investment fuel" that we discussed in Chapter 5.

6   https://www.jstor.org/stable/4478947

Average return ≈ (80%×10%)+(10%×4%)+(5%×9%)+(5%×2%) = 8%+0.4%+0.45%+0.1% = 8.95%

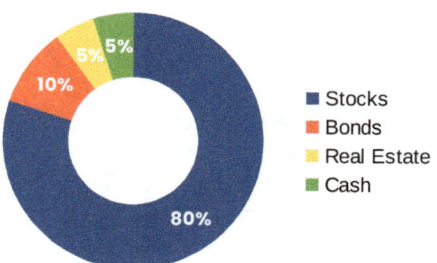

The model portfolio for the older investor could be expected to deliver nominal annual returns of ~7%. This would probably result in real returns closer to 4%, which is aligned with the "4% Rule", or the Rule of 25, that we discussed in Chapter 5.

Average return ≈ (50%×10%)+(40%×4%)+(5%×9%)+(5%×2%) = 5%+1.6%+0.45%+0.1% = 7.15%

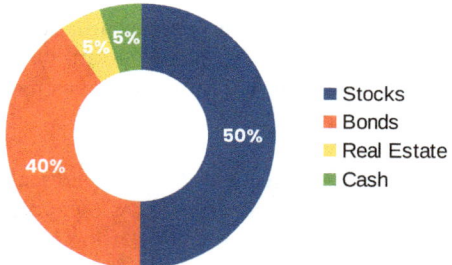

Of course these example allocations are not strict rules, but starting points for consideration. Investors should also be flexible and willing to adjust their allocations over time based on changes in the markets, their life circumstances, and whether they have some other passive income streams or not. For example, these could include social security or pension payments, a private business, or even royalties from books or music.

Other Considerations

Investing in startups is getting more popular, specially with crowdfunding sites and angel investing sites becoming more popular, more people are investing in this asset class. As already mentioned, with this asset class a few investors and funds make spectacular returns, and the majority underperform the stock market, or might even obtain negative returns. It is also a very illiquid asset class, as many startups take six to ten years to be mature enough for an exit. The author has invested very small amounts into more than fifty startups, with his portfolio already experiencing several startups going bankrupts or being bought for next to nothing, and a few successful exits at a higher valuation, but no "home run" investments yet. Despite having made the first investment more than seven years ago, he cannot tell at this points if he is going to end with an overall positive or negative return. For those adverturous enough to invest in startups, the advice we can share is to make it a tiny percentage of your overall investment portfolio, and then spread it into as many good opportunities as you can find. You should obviously filter opportunities where you notice "red flags", or that do not align with your values, or seem to overvalue the investment opportunity. However, it is important to know that startup returns tend to follow a power law distribution. If the opportunities you have access to are high-quality, it might have an n<2, which means that the more you spread your investment dollars into more opportunities, the higher the expected average return. That is why "dealflow" is so critical for VC funds, and they will try to look at as many quality investment opportunities as they can, even if they pass on most of them. This quirk from this type of power law distribution happens because it increases your chance of hitting a "home run". A guiding rule that some VC investors follow is to try to invest only in opportunities that could return the entire fund. In other words, if they are going to invest in 30 companies, they expect the startups to be promising enough to return 30x their invested capital. Legendary investor Peter Lynch has famously remarked that "all you need for a lifetime of successful investing is a few big winners, and the pluses from those will overwhelm the minuses from the stocks that don't work out". While he was talking about stock market investments, it seems to reflect the way many VC funds think and operate. Still, because of the illiquidity, lack of transparency, and high failure rate, we believe most investors should allocate an extremely small percentage of their funds to startups.

$$y = C x^{-n}$$

We have graphed a power law distribution with the constant C=1 and n = 1.5, this represents the probability of obtaining a given multiple on invested capital (MOIC). As can be seen, the probability of achieving a high MOIC decreases quite fast, but then shows a "fat tail", meaning it is relatively unlikely but still possible to generate gains in the thousands. We'll share a couple of stories that validate this is possible, even if quite unlikely. You also have to have a good network to help you get access to these opportunities.

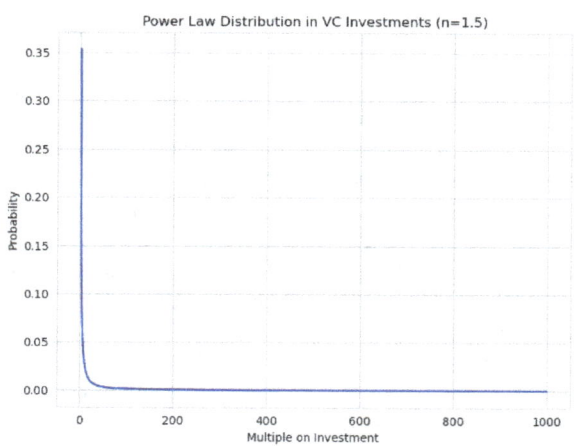

Notice how the likelihood of a complete loss is quite high. We will zoom in, so that we can see in more detail the "fat tail". The likelihood of making a 50x return according to this distribution is about 0.1%. Another thing to remember, is that even if you end up making a decent average MOIC, let's say 3x, it will probably take an average of around 10 years to exit the investments. This would result in compounded annual returns of only about 11%, not that different from what an astute stock market investor can make, without taking as much risk.

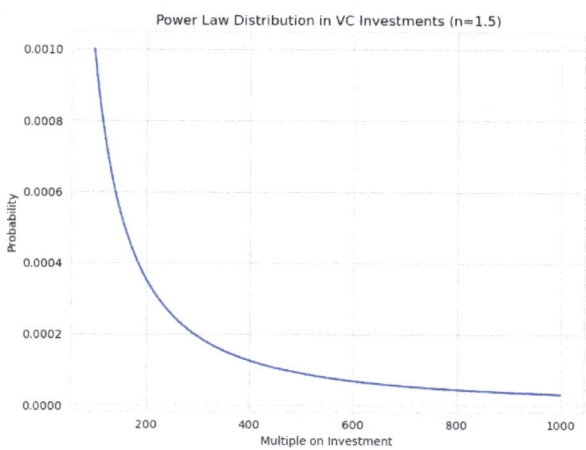

Remarkable Examples of High MOICs in Venture Capital and Angel Investing

Still, venture capital and angel investing are full of stories of extraordinary returns, some of which have become almost legendary. These examples highlight the extreme potential of power law dynamics in startup investing. One of the most celebrated examples is the initial angel investment in Google. In 1998, Andy Bechtolsheim, co-founder of Sun Microsystems, wrote a check for $100,000 to a then-unknown company named Google created by Larry Page and Sergey Brin, which had not even incorporated. This investment is now regarded as one of the most successful angel investments in history, yielding an astronomical return as Google evolved into the tech giant it is today.

Another iconic investment was made by Masayoshi Son, the founder of SoftBank. Over 23 years, SoftBank said it had turned an investment of 7.4 billion yen into 9.7 trillion yen, or roughly $54 million into $72 billion[7]. This resulted in a MOIC of over 1,300x, or a roughly 37% compounded annual return during the 23 years the investment lasted. This investment in the Chinese e-commerce platform represents one of the highest MOICs in venture capital history, and showcases the incredible impact of successful tech investments. These investments illustrate how a single, astute investment in a startup with immense potential can generate returns that far exceed the sum of many other investments, embodying the essence of the power law distribution in startup ecosystems.

The Unique Nature of Startup Investing

Investing in startups presents a markedly different scenario compared to estimating variables like the average height of a population. With physical characteristics like height, the law of large numbers applies – as you take more samples, the mean stabilizes and converges towards the true average of the population. This stability arises because human height follows a normal (Gaussian) distribution, where values are symmetrically clustered around a mean, and extreme values (very tall or very short individuals) have a minimal impact on the overall average.

In contrast, startup investing, especially in high-quality opportunities, often follows a power law distribution, particularly with an exponent $n<2$. This distribution is characterized by a 'heavy tail,' indicating that a significant portion of the total value comes from a small number of very high outcomes. In practical terms, this means that the average multiple on investment (MOIC) does not stabilize with more investments. Instead, it tends to increase as the number of investments grows. The reason is that each additional investment increases the probability of including an 'investment home run' – a startup that yields extraordinarily high returns.

This phenomenon is crucial in venture capital and startup investing. Unlike normal distributions, where adding more data points refines the mean, in power law distributions with $n<2$, more investments actually increase the expected average MOIC. This is because each new investment adds to the chances of hitting upon a wildly successful company, which, although

---

7   https://www.wsj.com/livecoverage/stock-market-today-dow-jones-05-11-2023/card/softbank-s-gain-on-alibaba-over-23-years-72-billion-mUstxx3qn5K41CZbFAvm

rare, can deliver outsized returns that dramatically lift the average MOIC of the entire investment portfolio.

As a result, in the world of startup investing, portfolio diversification doesn't just spread risk; it also enhances the possibility of encountering those rare, exceptionally high-return opportunities. This is fundamentally different from more conventional investment scenarios and highlights the unique risk-reward profile inherent in the startup ecosystem. It's a realm where a single extraordinary success can outweigh numerous failures, reshaping the investor's average returns as the portfolio size increases.

Cautionary Advice for Investors in Startups

While the potential for outsized returns in startup investing is undeniable, it is crucial for investors to remember that the majority of startups ultimately fail. The high-risk nature of investing in early-stage companies means that complete losses are far more common than windfall returns. This reality must be at the forefront of any investment strategy in this sector. Angel investing and crowdfunding, though potentially lucrative, should constitute only an extremely small percentage of an investor's overall portfolio. This conservative allocation is vital for risk management, ensuring that the potential failure of startup investments does not jeopardize one's overall financial stability.

Furthermore, within this allocated small percentage, diversification is key. Investors should aim to distribute their investment across a large number of startups. This approach aligns with the principles of power law distribution, where the likelihood of encountering a successful investment increases with the number of investments made. However, this strategy does not guarantee success; it merely increases the odds of including high-performing startups in one's portfolio. Therefore, investors must exercise due diligence, thoroughly researching each opportunity, while simultaneously managing their expectations and being prepared for the high probability of losses. Startup investing, with its unique blend of high risk and high reward, requires a balanced approach, combining optimism in the potential for groundbreaking success with a pragmatic understanding of the inherent risks involved.

Takeaways

The main takeaways for readers from this chapter are that there are many different types of fuels they can use for their financial independence rocket. It is important to understand their differences, and that a mix of the different asset classes is probably optimal. Stocks, bonds, and real estate should be the fundamental blocks for most investors, together with personal business or other passive income streams. While there is an opportunity cost to having a certain percentage allocate to cash, it also provides optionality in case a great investment opportunity arrives, or to cover an unexpected expense. Try to choose a mix that allows you to be comfortable with uncertainty, and not one that makes it difficult for you to sleep well at night.

It is also critical to remember that in most markets investors behave irrationally at times, be it with extreme optimism or extreme negativity. In these situations it is important to keep Buffett's advice in mind to "be fearful when others are greedy, and greedy when others are fearful". Finally, remember the importace of moats to protect profits, whether you are considering a business, a real estate property, or even a startup investment. Having a strong competitive advantage, or "moat", protects investment returns, and should be periodically evaluated. The strength of a business or property's moat is not static. Technological advancements, changes in consumer preferences, or innovative business models from competitors can all weaken an existing moat. For instance, the rise of e-commerce has challenged the moat of many brick-and-mortar retailers. Investors need to stay vigilant and reassess the strength of these moats regularly. A business that once held a dominant market position due to a particular technology or patent might lose its edge as new technologies emerge. Similarly, shifts in urban development or changes in infrastructure can affect the desirability of a real estate location. The dynamic nature of markets and technologies means that these advantages can erode over time. Investors who regularly assess and adapt to these changes can better protect their investments and capitalize on emerging opportunities. Keeping a pulse on market trends and competitor innovations is essential to ensure that today's strong moat doesn't become tomorrow's vulnerability.

Understanding and identifying business moats is crucial for investors looking for companies with sustainable competitive advantages. These moats not only protect the company but also ensure long-term profitability and investment returns. As Buffett and Munger have often emphasized, investing in companies with strong moats, at the right price, can lead to substantial long-term investment success.

Chapter 8: Micro-businesses and Passive Income

"Many of life's failures are people who did not realize how close they were to success when they gave up."
- Thomas Edison

While the main engine accelerating the rocket towards financial escape velocity will be the investment portfolio, at least for most people, passive income streams can serve as additional booster engines that can help you attain financial independence faster. They also provide added stability and diversification, and in some cases could grow spectacularly. Things that started as hobbies or passion projects sometimes become widely successful businesses. The beauty of passive income is that once it's established, it can continue to generate money with minimal active effort. This chapter explores the various facets of generating passive income, particularly through micro-businesses and intellectual property (IP), and provides insights into effective monetization strategies, mental models like TRIZ for idea generation, and the importance of negotiation skills to obtain fair value from your innovations.

The digital age has transformed the landscape of passive income generation, particularly for creative endeavors. In today's interconnected world, the ability to create and distribute digital products – from software to music and graphic designs – has opened up unprecedented opportunities for individuals to develop streams of passive income. One of the most significant advantages of digital products is their ease of reproduction and distribution. Unlike physical goods, digital items can be duplicated countless times at almost no additional cost. This characteristic dramatically changes the economics of production and sales. For instance, a software developer can create a piece of software once and sell it to thousands, if not millions, of customers without worrying about the costs of materials or shipping. Similarly, a graphic designer can create a design and sell it as a digital product, such as a downloadable file or a template, across the globe with minimal overhead costs.

Online platforms have further simplified the process of reaching a global audience. Websites like Amazon for self-published authors, Bandcamp for musicians, and Etsy for artists and designers, provide accessible marketplaces where creators can showcase and sell their digital products. These platforms handle many of the logistical aspects, such as payment processing and digital delivery, allowing creators to focus more on their craft and less on the intricacies of the business side.

The first step, of course, is getting an original idea. For that you can follow the example of Masayoshi Son, SoftBank's founder. We already talked about his impressive investment in Alibaba, but how did he get the money to get started in business and investing? When he was a student at Berkely he decided to allocate a few minutes every day to generating potential invention ideas. As he tells the story, he "...had 250 inventions that I wrote down in my 'Invention Idea Notes.' Then I picked one to develop a prototype and apply for a patent. I made close to $1 million by selling the patent to Sharp."[8] It was a really good idea, an electronic pocket language translator, but he did not have all the technical skills to develop a prototype

---

8   https://hbr.org/1992/01/japanese-style-entrepreneurship-an-interview-with-softbanks-ceo-masayoshi-son

himself. So he hired some of his professors, and paid them for their work once he sold the patent to Sharp. Notice how he did not go with his first idea, but instead he carefully evaluated the merits of each of them before committing to one. In fact he used a similar process before deciding to enter the personal computer software business. He used about 25 measurements to evaluate the 40 business ideas he had. It was not an obvious business, but sometimes original ideas that are quickly dismissed by other turn out to be some of the best ones.

> If you go back to 1981, everything wasn't so obvious. The PC was only a toy then. There was some hardware already made in Japan, but there was almost no software. Nobody even knew what kind of software was available in all of Japan. - Masayoshi Son

Another example of a business idea that was ridiculed by some at first is Airbnb. People thought that renting a room to strangers in your house was a really bad idea. Turns out, it was a good idea that looked bad on the surface. Sometimes these are the best ideas because you encounter less competition, and by the time you prove that the idea actually works you have a significant lead over the competition.

Not every idea has to become a multi-billion dollar company, our main objective is to find ideas that create passive income. Some of them will be niche ideas, and that is completely fine. An example the author found while building a website was a favicon generator. Favicons are special images that you see on tabs when using an internet browser. Creating a favicon images requires a number of steps and having image editing software. The author found a free site that automated the creation of favicon images, and was free to use, only asking for a donation if you found it helpful. Since it saved the author some valuable time, he was happy to mae a small donation to thank the tool creator.

The Value of Intellectual Property

There are a number of areas where it is particularly easy to create passive income streams, these include the following digital products and intellectual property:

- Software: Software, including mobile apps and SaaS (Software as a Service) products, represents one of the most lucrative areas for digital passive income. Once developed, these products require minimal ongoing costs, while the potential customer base is enormous. Examples include productivity tools, educational apps, games, and specialized software solutions.

- Music: With streaming services like Spotify and Apple Music, musicians can reach a global audience without the need for physical distribution. Royalties from streaming and digital downloads provide a steady income stream.

- E-books and Online Courses: The rise of e-books and online courses has revolutionized the publishing and education industries. Authors can self-publish without the need for traditional publishing houses, and educators can create and sell courses on platforms like Udemy and Skillshare.

- Graphic Designs and Photography: Websites like Shutterstock and Adobe Stock allow graphic designers and photographers to sell their creations to a broad audience. Once uploaded, these works can continue to generate income as they are licensed and downloaded by users worldwide.

- Patents and other forms of IP: There are two main types of patents, utility patents (which are people think of usually when they here the word patent) which cover new inventions, and design patents which cover how something is designed. Other common intellectual property assets include tradesecrets, copyrights, and trademarks. We'll talk more about how to protect your ideas using these tools later in the chapter. We'll just mention a few examples, like when celebrities trademark their names and then make licensing deals with perfume manufacturers. If someone comes up with a popular superhero character, that can be protected by copyrights too, and then licensed to movie studios, toy makers, etc. Some of your favorite super hero characters are valued at billions of dollars.

In the next few pages we'll share examples of people that famously created valuable assets from their ideas, many of them living from royalties from patents, music, lyrics, fictional characters, books, etc. In some cases the IP assets have continued generating income even after the creator passed away, benefitting their families or chosen charities for a long time. In some cases the creators leveraged the intellectual property to create businesses or complete franchises that are even more valuable. These stories illustrate that great ideas can come from anyone, anywhere. The common thread among these individuals is the ability to recognize a problem or need, devise a creative solution, and then have the determination to bring their idea to market.

- Tim and Nina Zagat: The Zagats were lawyers who started compiling restaurant reviews from friends as a hobby. This led to the creation of the Zagat Survey, a restaurant guide that gained immense popularity. Google eventually acquired Zagat, turning a simple idea into a lucrative business.

- Sara Blakely: Working as a salesperson and occasionally doing stand-up comedy, Blakely came up with the idea for Spanx, a brand of footless pantyhose. She invested her life savings to develop the product, which eventually turned into a billion-dollar business, making her one of the most successful self-made women entrepreneurs.

- John Osher: Osher developed the SpinBrush, an affordable electric toothbrush, while running a small business. Procter & Gamble bought his company for $475 million, showcasing how a practical invention can lead to a significant financial windfall.

- Joy Mangano: A single mother of three, Mangano invented the Miracle Mop, a self-wringing mop, which she initially sold out of her car. Her invention became popular after a successful pitch on QVC and led to a multimillion-dollar business, inspiring the movie "Joy."

- Gary Dahl: An advertising executive, Dahl jokingly created the "Pet Rock" as a low-maintenance pet alternative. The product became a cultural sensation in the 1970s, making Dahl a millionaire.

- Pierre Omidyar: Omidyar, a computer programmer, started eBay as a personal project. It rapidly grew into one of the world's largest online auction sites, turning him into a billionaire.

- George de Mestral: Velcro's hook-and-loop fastener patent was simple yet revolutionary. Velcro Industries makes hundreds of millions in sales annually, showcasing the patent's value. The inspiration came from a walk outdoors where burrs had attached to him and his dog. The invention became popular when NASA used it to maintain objects attached to walls while floating in orbit.

- Catherine Hettinger: Catherine created the original design of the fidget spinner as a way to entertain her daughter. She let the patent lapse due to renewal costs. The fidget spinner later became a global craze, showing the potential lost revenue.

- Robert Kearns: Kearns, a college professor, invented the intermittent windshield wiper system after an injury impaired his vision. After a lengthy legal battle, he successfully sued Ford and Chrysler for patent infringement, receiving millions in compensation.

- Thomas Edison: The famous inventor held over 1,000 patents, including those for the electric light bulb and the phonograph. The royalties and income from these patents not only provided Edison with a substantial income during his lifetime but also continued to benefit his estate long after his passing.

- George Lucas: The creator of "Star Wars" sold his company, Lucasfilm, to Disney, but not before he negotiated a deal that included a percentage of the earnings from future "Star Wars" films, merchandise, and theme park attractions, ensuring a continuous flow of income.

- Agatha Christie: The famed mystery writer's estate continues to earn royalties from her extensive catalog of novels, plays, and the film and television adaptations of her works. Her books have sold billions of copies and remain popular worldwide.

- J.R.R. Tolkien: The estate of J.R.R. Tolkien, the author of "The Lord of the Rings" and "The Hobbit," has benefited greatly from the royalties of book sales, as well as the immensely successful film adaptations and merchandise related to his Middle-earth universe.

- Charles Schulz: The creator of the "Peanuts" comic strip, Charles Schulz, passed away in 2000, but his estate continues to earn significant income from licensing deals, including the use of his characters in advertisements, merchandise, and the popular "Peanuts" holiday television specials.

- George Carlin: The late comedian George Carlin, known for his influential stand-up routines, left behind a body of work that continues to generate income. His performances, recordings, and book royalties continue to provide earnings for his estate.

There are also many solopreneurs and artists/designers who have turned their unique ideas into sustainable, financial successes. These individuals often leverage their creativity, skills, and the power of digital platforms to build a livelihood around their passions. Here are some examples:

- Amanda Hocking: An early success story in self-publishing, Hocking wrote and self-published her paranormal romance novels as e-books. Without the backing of a traditional publisher, she sold millions of copies and made millions of dollars, proving the potential of digital self-publishing.

- Etsy Crafters: Many artists and crafters have turned to platforms like Etsy to sell their handmade goods. For example, Alicia Shaffer became one of Etsy's top sellers with her store, ThreeBirdNest, selling handmade knitwear and accessories. Her store generates substantial income, showcasing how digital marketplaces can turn hobbies into profitable businesses.

- YouTube Creators: YouTube has enabled numerous creators to earn a living through their video content. One of the author's favorite channels is 3Blue1Brown which was created by Grant Sanderson to explain a variety of topics in math, physics and computer science, with an emphasis on visualizing the core ideas. It shows that even subjects considered less popular can result in massive audiences.

- App Developers: Independent app developers have found success by creating unique mobile apps. Marco Arment, the creator of Instapaper and Overcast, is a notable example. He developed popular apps as a one-person operation and successfully monetized them.

- Webcomic Artists: Artists like Randall Munroe of "xkcd" and Sarah Andersen of "Sarah's Scribbles" have turned their webcomics into full-time careers. They earn money through book sales, merchandise, and speaking engagements.

- Indie Game Developers: Independent game developers like Eric Barone, who created the hit game "Stardew Valley," have made successful careers by developing and selling their games. Barone created "Stardew Valley" by himself and it became a best-seller, demonstrating the potential for indie developers in the gaming industry.

These examples reflect a diverse range of paths to financial success as a solopreneur or artist/designer. They highlight the importance of leveraging digital platforms, building a personal brand, and connecting directly with an audience or market. There are many more examples of individuals and small teams who have turned their ideas into successful ventures. Here are a few additional examples:

- Markus Frind: Markus Frind, the developer of the dating website Plenty of Fish, is a notable example of a successful solopreneur. He created the site in 2003 and initially ran it independently from his apartment. The website became hugely popular and was eventually sold for $575 million in 2015.

- Ermal Fraze: Ermal Fraze invented the pull-tab mechanism for aluminum cans, revolutionizing beverage packaging. He founded the Dayton Reliable Tool Company to manufacture these pull tabs, which became standard in the industry. In a cell phone interview while he was on his yacht, his son Terry Fraze was asked how much his family had made from the self-opening can. He replied the same way his father used to by saying "I did pretty well for a farm boy." Their company Dayton Reliable Tool reported $50 million in revenue and had 500 employees in 1980.

- Patty Hill and Mildred J. Hill: The "Happy Birthday to You" song, often attributed to Patty and Mildred Hill, has been a subject of copyright controversy. Originally composed as "Good Morning to All," the song's melody was later used with the "Happy Birthday" lyrics. Warner/Chappell Music claimed ownership of the song for years, collecting royalties, until a 2016 court ruling declared the song to be in the public domain.

- Alex Tew - The Million Dollar Homepage: In 2005, Alex Tew, a student from England, created The Million Dollar Homepage, where he sold 1 million pixels on a web page for $1 each to fund his university education. The idea quickly went viral, and Tew successfully made $1 million, demonstrating the power of unique and simple online business concepts.

- Julie Deane - The Cambridge Satchel Company: Julie Deane started The Cambridge Satchel Company with just £600 to pay for her children's school fees. She designed and created stylish satchels that became a fashion sensation, leading to a multimillion-pound business.

- Richard T. James - Slinky: In 1943, mechanical engineer Richard T. James invented the Slinky by accident. This simple toy became a cultural icon, selling over 300 million units worldwide and generating ongoing income for the James family.

These stories demonstrate the diverse ways in which individuals have capitalized on their ideas, creativity, and the power of digital platforms to build successful businesses and generate income. From inventors and musicians to tech entrepreneurs, each narrative offers unique insights into the potential of small-scale ideas to achieve significant impact.

More recently, crowdfunding platforms like Kickstarter and Indiegogo have become launchpads for many innovative products and ideas. These stories highlight how crowdfunding platforms have democratized the process of bringing innovative ideas to the market, allowing creators to directly connect with potential customers and investors. They showcase the potential of crowdfunding in validating and kickstarting new products and businesses. Some the success stories that started as ideas in these platforms include:

- Pebble Smartwatch - Kickstarter: One of the most famous Kickstarter success stories, the Pebble Smartwatch, raised over $10 million in 2012. It was one of the first smartwatches to gain widespread popularity, paving the way for the smart wearable industry.

- Coolest Cooler - Kickstarter: The Coolest Cooler, which featured a blender, waterproof Bluetooth speakers, and a USB charger, raised over $13 million on Kickstarter. It became one of the highest-funded campaigns on the platform, showcasing the potential of combining practicality with innovation.

- BauBax Travel Jacket - Kickstarter: This travel jacket came with 15 features like a neck pillow, eye mask, gloves, and various pockets designed for travelers. It raised over $9 million on Kickstarter, tapping into the niche market of travel gear.

- Oculus Rift - Kickstarter: Before being acquired by Facebook, Oculus Rift started as a Kickstarter project that raised $2.4 million. It played a significant role in revitalizing interest in virtual reality.

- Flow Hive - Indiegogo: Flow Hive, a revolutionary beehive invention, allows honey to be harvested directly from the hive without opening it. It raised over $13 million on Indiegogo, demonstrating the public's interest in innovative and sustainable solutions.

- Anova Precision Cooker - Kickstarter: Anova Culinary's Precision Cooker, a device for sous vide cooking, was successfully funded on Kickstarter. It became popular among cooking enthusiasts and helped bring sous vide cooking to more home kitchens.

- Tile - Selfstarter: Tile, a small Bluetooth tracker to help find lost items, originally launched on Selfstarter (an open-source crowdfunding platform) and later moved to its website for pre-orders. It became immensely popular for its practicality and simplicity.

However, it is not just inventors and entrepreneurs that can create very significant passive income by creating intellectual property assets. Some creatives might not be as famous as the artists that use their work, but many song writers and music composers earn significant royalties. Photographers, designers, and artists can also find ways to generative income from their craft. Some good examples include:

- Max Martin: A Swedish songwriter and producer, Max Martin has written or co-written numerous hit songs for artists like Britney Spears, Taylor Swift, and The Weeknd. His songwriting royalties have made him one of the most successful songwriters in pop music history.

- Diane Warren: An American songwriter, Warren has penned a vast number of hits for artists ranging from Celine Dion to Aerosmith. She earns substantial royalties from her extensive catalog of songs.

- Carol Kaye: A prolific session musician and bass guitarist, Kaye also wrote numerous lines and riffs for famous songs. Her contributions to iconic tracks continue to earn her royalties.

- Annie Leibovitz: One of the most well-known photographers in the world, Leibovitz has made a significant income from her photography, including portrait work for numerous celebrities and high-profile publications.

- Substack Writers: Various writers on Substack, a newsletter publishing platform, have successfully monetized their newsletters. By focusing on niche topics or unique perspectives, they've attracted paid subscribers, turning newsletter writing into a viable source of income.

Each of these individuals demonstrates the potential of earning a living through creative talents, be it in songwriting, photography, or content creation. Their success stories highlight how intellectual property, in various forms, can be a sustainable source of income, especially when it resonates with a wide audience. Just remember to properly protect your valuable ideas with copyrights, trademarks, patents, and trade secrets. Having strong IP protection will make it a lot easier to negotiate deals and obtain royalties or other benefits from your ideas and creations.

In the next sections we will se some methods to help generate original ideas. One is using ideas from one domain to solve problems in a different field. The other is using fundamental principles that have been found by analyzing thousands of patents.

Cross-Domain Innovations: Bridging Ideas for Revolutionary Breakthroughs

The concept of cross-domain innovation, where ideas from one field are applied to solve problems in another, has been a catalyst for some of the most groundbreaking advancements in history. This approach often leads to innovative solutions that traditional, domain-specific thinking might overlook. By transcending the boundaries of conventional knowledge, these cross-pollinations of ideas can spark revolutionary innovations.

A quintessential example of this is Hedy Lamarr, an Austrian-American actress and inventor. Lamarr is best known for her work in Hollywood during its Golden Age, but her most enduring legacy is perhaps her contribution to wireless communication technology. In the midst of World War II, Lamarr co-invented a frequency-hopping spread spectrum technology, initially intended to prevent the jamming of radio-controlled torpedoes.

Drawing on her knowledge of music, Lamarr conceptualized the idea of rapidly switching frequencies in a synchronized pattern, akin to the unpredictable jumps in a piano keyboard's notes. This invention was a significant departure from her expertise in acting, yet her understanding of musical rhythms and patterns provided a unique perspective that was groundbreaking in the field of communications technology.

While her invention was not immediately adopted by the military, it laid the foundational principles for modern spread-spectrum communication technology. Today, Lamarr's frequency hopping is a cornerstone of wireless technologies like Bluetooth, Wi-Fi, and GPS. It exemplifies how transferring knowledge from the arts to technology can lead to innovations that shape the future.

Lamarr's story is a powerful reminder of the potential that lies in interdisciplinary thinking. It encourages innovators and problem-solvers to look beyond the confines of their specialized fields and draw inspiration from seemingly unrelated domains. This kind of thinking can lead to solutions that are not only novel but also revolutionary in their impact!

TRIZ: Harnessing Fundamental Principles for Innovation

The creation of the TRIZ innovation framework is a fascinating example of how the analysis of commonalities across various patents can lead to powerful methodologies for problem-solving and innovation. TRIZ, a Russian acronym for "Theory of Inventive Problem Solving," was developed by Soviet inventor and science fiction writer Genrich Altshuller and his colleagues in the 1940s. The genesis of TRIZ was in Altshuller's realization that despite the diversity of patents and inventions, there were underlying patterns and principles that frequently recurred.

Altshuller and his team embarked on a comprehensive study of hundreds of thousands of patents and discovered that many innovative solutions could be categorized into a relatively small set of principles. They identified that inventive problems and their solutions were often repeated across industries and sciences, revealing that the process of innovation could be systematically distilled and taught.

TRIZ operates on the premise that the best solutions resolve contradictions without compromising between two extremes. It provides a structured approach to problem-solving, which is contrary to the common belief that innovation requires a purely intuitive or spontaneous mindset. The methodology is built around several key concepts, including the 40 Inventive Principles, the Contradiction Matrix, and the concept of Ideality.

The 40 Inventive Principles are general strategies derived from patterns observed in inventive solutions. These principles offer different ways to approach and solve problems, encouraging thinkers to look beyond the conventional solutions. An example of these principles is "nesting", which computer programmers will recognize in the use of "for loops" inside other "for loops". The principle of nesting can also be visualized in the design of traffic cones, which use the principle of nesting for efficient stacking and storing. Another example of a TRIZ invention principle is "counter-weight", which is used for example in elevators to counter the weight of the cabin, so that the motor only has to spend energy moving the people inside. Other examples of invention principles include "asymmetry", "taking a preliminary action", and "change of color". If you visit the TRIZ Wikipedia page, https://en.wikipedia.org/wiki/TRIZ, you will find a wonderful image iwith the 40 principles and graphic illustrations of examples of each. Another great resource is the website TRIZ40, https://www.triz40.com, which has a tool that allows you to define the contradiction you are trying to solve, and lists the principles most likely to result in an innovation that solves the problem. It makes use of the Contradiction Matrix, which helps identify the most relevant principles to resolve specific technical contradictions in a given problem. Using the elevator example, in "feature to improve" you would select "power" as we want to use less power to operate the elevator, and in "feature to preserve" you would select "weight of moving object". It is a contradiction because we want to reduce the power needed to move the elevator, without making a sacrifice in reducing its weight. When you click "browse the Triz Matrix" one of the invention principles it suggest looking into is "anti-weight" which is how elevator manufacturers typically solve that problem. The suggested principles will not always be relevant, but they are a great place to start brainstorming for innovative solutions.

The concept of Ideality is also used in the TRIZ framework, and it focuses on maximizing the desired functions of a system while minimizing any harmful or undesired effects.

TRIZ's beauty lies in its applicability across different fields and problems. It's not limited to engineering or technical disciplines but can be used in business, software development, social sciences, and more. By applying TRIZ, innovators can systematically explore all possible solutions to a problem, even those that might not be immediately apparent. It encourages looking at problems from new angles, leading to more creative and effective solutions.

In essence, TRIZ provides a roadmap for thinking outside the box, enabling practitioners to generate innovative solutions systematically. Its foundation in the analysis of a vast array of patents demonstrates the richness of ideas that can be gleaned from existing solutions, serving as an inspiration well for solving new, complex problems. The TRIZ framework is a testament to the power of structured, analytical thinking in the creative process of innovation.

The Art of Monetization and Pricing

In the journey of transforming an invention, artistic work, or creative idea into a financial success, understanding the art of monetization and pricing is crucial. This process involves not only determining how to make money from your creation but also how much to charge. For many inventors, artists, and creatives, royalties from licensing agreements are a primary means of monetization.

Negotiating royalties requires a deep understanding of the value of your intellectual property and the market standards. When entering into a licensing agreement, several factors should be considered:

- Royalty rates can vary significantly across different industries. For instance, in publishing, authors typically receive royalties between 5% and 15% of the book's selling price. In the music industry, royalties can range from 8% to 15% for physical media and around 10% to 25% for digital downloads. Patented inventions in technology or manufacturing may see royalties anywhere from 2% to 10% of the wholesale price. It's crucial to research and understand the standard rates in your specific industry.

- Evaluate the uniqueness, market demand, and potential profitability of your IP. Stronger, more unique, or highly demanded IP can command higher royalty rates.

- When negotiating, consider not just the percentage but also the base from which the royalty is calculated. Be clear about whether it's from the retail price, wholesale price, or net profits. Also, consider negotiating advance payments, minimum annual royalties, or performance clauses to ensure a baseline income.

Aside from royalties, there are other ways to monetize creative work:

- Lump-Sum Payments: In some cases, particularly if ongoing management of royalties seems complex or uncertain, accepting a one-time payment might be preferable.

- Profit-Sharing Models: This can be an alternative to traditional royalties, especially in collaborative projects or startups.

- Merchandising and Ancillary Rights: Particularly relevant in the entertainment and literary industries, where characters or concepts can be licensed for merchandise, adaptations, or spin-offs.

A crucial aspect of successful negotiation, especially when discussing royalties, licensing agreements, or the sale of intellectual property, is understanding and leveraging fundamental negotiating concepts such as BATNA (Best Alternative to a Negotiated Agreement) and ZOPA (Zone of Possible Agreement).

Your BATNA is essentially your backup plan or the best course of action if the current negotiation fails. Knowing your BATNA provides a clear understanding of when to walk away from a negotiation. It empowers you to make better decisions and helps in maintaining a strong negotiating position. For instance, if an artist is negotiating royalties for their music with a record label, their BATNA could be self-publishing or seeking alternative labels. A strong BATNA not only boosts your confidence but can also positively influence the terms of the negotiation, as it reduces the likelihood of accepting unfavorable conditions.

ZOPA represents the range in which an agreement is acceptable to both parties. It's the overlap between what each party is willing to accept. Understanding the ZOPA is crucial for reaching a mutually beneficial agreement. If the ZOPA is non-existent, it means no deal can be made. During negotiations, both parties often explore each other's interests and limits to accurately identify the ZOPA. For instance, in licensing negotiations, if an inventor wants a minimum of 5% in royalties and the licensee is willing to pay up to 10%, the ZOPA lies between 5% and 10%.

Other Negotiating Fundamentals:

- Preparation and Research: Adequate preparation, including understanding the other party's needs, constraints, and goals, is vital.

- Effective Communication: Clearly articulating your position and understanding the other party's points can lead to more productive negotiations.

- Emotional Intelligence: The ability to manage emotions and understand emotional cues from the other party is crucial in negotiations.

- Win-Win Mindset: Successful negotiations often involve finding solutions that benefit both parties, rather than approaching the negotiation as a zero-sum game.

In conclusion, a deep understanding of BATNA, ZOPA, and other negotiation fundamentals is essential for anyone looking to successfully navigate the complexities of royalty negotiations, licensing deals, or any form of business agreement. These concepts not only facilitate more effective negotiations but also ensure that the outcomes are favorable and sustainable for all parties involved.

Pricing Considerations

Some times it will not be possible to find someone willing to commercialize or monetize your idea, at least not based on terms you believe are fair. If you are convinced the idea is good and you truly believe in it, you can take the step of commercializing it yourself. One of the most important decisions you will have to make is determining the optimal price. Determining the right price for your product, service, or licensing deal is as much an art as a science. Several key factors should be considered:

- Cost-Based Pricing: Calculate the total cost of producing your product or service and add a markup for profit. This approach is straightforward but may not always capture the product's perceived value.

- Market-Based Pricing: Look at similar products or services in the market to gauge an appropriate price point. This requires understanding your competitors and the market demand.

- Value-Based Pricing: Price based on the perceived or estimated value to the customer. This can often lead to higher profit margins but requires a deep understanding of your customer's needs and the value your product provides.

Sometimes, the most effective pricing strategy can be counterintuitive, such as setting the price at zero and monetizing through alternative means. Offering a product or service for free can be a powerful tool in certain contexts. The 'freemium' model, widely used in the software industry, involves offering a basic version of a product for free while charging for advanced features. This strategy can attract a large user base, some of whom will eventually pay for additional functionalities. In other cases, a product is offered for free to gain a wide audience, and revenue is generated through advertising, sponsorships, or data monetization. For example, social media platforms and online publications often use this model to great effect.

Pricing can often have counterintuitive effects on consumer behavior. One notable phenomenon is that, in some cases, increasing prices can actually boost sales. This can occur because high prices are often associated with high quality. Consumers might perceive a more expensive product as superior, thereby enhancing its appeal.

For example, luxury goods often see increased demand as their prices rise, as the high cost enhances their status symbol appeal. Similarly, in the wine industry, higher-priced bottles are frequently perceived as being of better quality, regardless of the actual taste. This psychological association between price and quality can lead consumers to value and enjoy a product more when it's priced higher

More advanced pricing techniques like Dutch auctions, where the price is gradually lowered until a buyer is found, can be particularly effective in finding the market's highest willingness to pay. This method is often used for unique items, such as art or collectibles. Additionally, experimenting with different price points can yield valuable insights into consumer behavior. Businesses can test various prices in different markets or time periods to determine the optimal price for maximizing profits or market penetration.

Market segmentation is also a great strategy for optimizing profits. Different consumer segments may have varying levels of price sensitivity and purchasing power. By creating slightly different versions of a product or service, a business can cater to different segments effectively. For example, a software company might offer a basic version for price-sensitive consumers, a professional version with advanced features for power users, and an enterprise version with additional support and customization options for corporate clients. This approach allows businesses to capture a larger portion of the market by addressing the specific needs and price points of different customer groups.

Whether employing a free-to-premium model, leveraging auction mechanisms, conducting price experiments, or utilizing segmentation, the goal is to find a pricing strategy that aligns with both the value proposition of the product or service and the needs of the target market. By doing so, businesses can effectively monetize their offerings while meeting or even exceeding their customers' expectations.

The art of monetization and pricing is a critical skill for inventors, artists, and creatives seeking to profit from their innovations. Understanding how to negotiate royalties, what percentages are appropriate, and other monetization strategies, along with pricing your offering correctly, are key components of financial success in the creative and innovative realms. By mastering these elements, creators can ensure that they are adequately compensated for their intellectual contributions.

Take Aways

We shared many examples of people that were successful monetizing a great idea, and these covered a wide array of creative endeavors that transformed into lucrative businesses or income streams. They illustrate that with innovation, determination, and a unique idea, it's possible to create substantial passive income or royalties in various fields.

It is important to remember Masayoshi Son and his list of hundreds of ideas. Not every idea will be good, and you have to properly test and evaluate them. Also remember that it might take more time and effort to go from idea to a functioning prototype or a finished book. When you feel like you hit a roadblock, remember Thomas Edison's quote: "Nearly every man who develops an idea works it up to the point where it looks impossible, and then gets discouraged. That's not the place to become discouraged." To create a successful passive income stream you will need persistence and resilience. Also remember the story of the fidget spinner, where the inventor was not able to collect royalties as a result of the decision of not paying the renewal fee. Make sure to understand the details of copyright, patent, and trademark law where you live.

Finally, go take advantage of the of the wonderful opportunities the digital world and many popular platforms have created to reach global audiences, and turn your creative ideas into a source of passive income.

Chapter 9: Sustainable Finance

"What you do makes a difference, and you have to decide what kind of difference you want to make." - Jane Goodall

Sustainable finance refers to financial investments made with the intention of generating positive, measurable social and environmental impact alongside a financial return. It reflects a growing trend where investors seek to align their financial goals with their personal values.

Impact investing focuses on investments that can deliver tangible social or environmental benefits. ESG principles are a set of criteria used to screen potential investments based on their environmental, social, and governance practices. Investing in line with personal values can influence industries by affecting their cost of capital. By avoiding investments in controversial industries like gambling, tobacco, and arms, investors can indirectly discourage these sectors. Even companies in generally positive industries can engage in harmful practices, such as pollution, unfair treatment of customers or workers, or producing dangerous products. Investors are increasingly using resources like Wikipedia, Trustpilot, and Glassdoor to research a company's reputation and ethical practices.

Companies that behave responsibly towards society and the environment often have more honest management, which can lead to better long-term returns for investors. Ethical behavior reduces the risk of government fines and regulation and is beneficial for brand image. For example, Patagonia's commitment to sustainability has significantly contributed to its success.

Corporate Knights publishes the Global 100 index annually, listing highly regarded companies in terms of sustainable practices. This index has consistently outperformed many stock market indices, highlighting the potential financial benefits of sustainable investing.[9]

The Story of Patagonia

Patagonia, founded by Yvon Chouinard, stands as a testament to the power of aligning business with environmental stewardship. Chouinard's deep concern for the environment drove him to ensure that Patagonia operated sustainably. This commitment ranged from using organic materials to advocating for environmental causes.

This ethos deeply resonated with consumers, who were drawn not just to the products, but to the company's values. As a result, Patagonia saw significant financial success, becoming more than just a brand, but a symbol of environmental activism in commerce.

In a remarkable move, Chouinard recently donated the company to a trust and a nonprofit organization dedicated to fighting climate change. This decision ensures that the profits are used to combat the environmental crisis, making the planet better for all. Through this act, Patagonia's success now directly contributes to broader environmental efforts, embodying the ideal of business as a force for good.

Impact Investing and ESG Reports

Sustainable finance is not just about avoiding harm, but actively seeking to do good through investment choices. It represents a holistic approach to investing, considering the broader impact of where money is invested. Think of the trillions of dollars that will have to be invested to transition the world energy infrastructure to clean technologies in order to avoid the worst effects of climate change. This is a big challenge, but also a great growth investing opportunity. Investors are rewarding renewable energy produces with higher valuation multiples compared to traditional energy companies, as they have a lot more growth potential.

Many companies now publish ESG reports on their investor websites, detailing their environmental, social, and governance practices. When analyzing these reports, investors should look for key elements:

- Specific Goals and Progress: Look for clearly defined ESG goals and the progress made towards these objectives. Vague statements are less valuable than specific targets and achievements.

- Third-party Audits and Certifications: Credibility is enhanced when reports are verified by independent third parties or include recognized certifications.

---

9   https://www.corporateknights.com/leadership/2021-global-100-progress-report/

- Alignment with Global Standards: Check if the company aligns its reporting with global ESG standards, such as the Global Reporting Initiative or the Sustainability Accounting Standards Board.

- Transparency and Challenges: A trustworthy ESG report will also discuss challenges and areas for improvement, demonstrating the company's commitment to transparency and ongoing development in ESG practices.

These reports are a valuable tool for understanding a company's commitment to ESG principles, but it's important to critically assess their content for authenticity and depth.

It is important to evaluate sustainability aspects when doing due dilligence for bonds as well. This also affects a company's cost of capital, and therefore you can have a positive or negative impact here as well. A specific type of bond was invented to finance particularly important sustainability initiatives, these are called green bonds. They were designed to fund projects that have positive environmental and climate benefits. The proceeds from these bonds are exclusively applied to projects like renewable energy, energy efficiency, sustainable waste management, and clean transportation.

Shareholder activism is also important if you want to be a sustainable investor. As a shareholder you get to vote on innitiatives that play a crucial role in steering companies towards sustainable practices. Investors can influence corporate behavior by exercising their rights as shareholders to vote on sustainability-related matters or by engaging directly with company management to advocate for ESG-focused changes.

The future of sustainable finance looks promising as it becomes increasingly mainstream. Trends suggest a growing emphasis on integrating ESG factors into all aspects of financial analysis, leading to more sustainable global economic growth models. Different countries have varying regulations affecting ESG investing, which can either promote or hinder the growth of sustainable finance. Understanding these legal frameworks is crucial for investors looking to engage in sustainable investing.

While ESG investing is gaining popularity, it faces criticisms like greenwashing, where companies exaggerate their sustainability efforts. Investors need to be diligent in verifying ESG claims and understand the complexities involved in measuring true sustainability impacts.

Chapter 10 - Optimal Stopping Strategies

"An investment in knowledge pays the best interest." – Benjamin Franklin

Optimal stopping theory, a fascinating field within decision theory and statistics, aims to determine the best time to take a specific action to try achieve the best possible outcome. This discipline has evolved to offer practical solutions in various domains, including finance and everyday life decisions. Maximize the probability of making a correct decision. Bad timing can be ruinous, as Theodore Hill explains in an excellent article in *American Scientist*, and understanding the principles behind optimal stopping can help improve even mundane undertakings such as searching for a better parking space, deciding to accept a job offer, hiring a new eployee, or scheduling retirement.[10]

Decisions have to be made, sometimes with partial information or uncertainty regarding some variables. Based with the available information, one has to make a decision while trying to optimize the outcome. Using strategies based on probability principles, it is sometimes possible to improve the odds of making the right choice. An applied mathematician named Richard Bellman invented dynamic programming to obtain optimal strategies to many stopping problems. In some cases, simpler tools can be used that offer practical and powerful solutions.

One of the best know is the 37% rule, or 1/e where e is Euler's number and approximately 2.71828, and guarantees making the best choice more than one third of the time, regardless of the number of options available. One example application would be when purchasing a house, the theory suggests reviewing 37% of the options without commitment, and then choosing the first one that surpasses all previously seen properties. In practical terms this could mean that if you are willing to visit ten candidate houses, automatically discard the first four options, and then purchase the first one that surpasses all the first four.

---

10 "Knowing When to Stop" By Theodore Hill
    https://www.americanscientist.org/article/knowing-when-to-stop

Optimal stopping theory beautifully aligns with the adage of being "in the right place at the right time." This concept emphasizes the importance of timing in decision-making, whether it's in business, investing, or personal choices. Just like the ideal of catching the perfect opportunity relies on a blend of preparation and timing, optimal stopping involves assessing current situations and determining the most advantageous moment to act. It's about strategically waiting for that opportune moment and then seizing it with decisiveness. Just as a surfer waits for the right wave that will provide the best ride, in life and business, it's about identifying and catching the 'right wave' of opportunity.

The concept of "search versus exploitation" intricately ties into the principles of optimal stopping, providing another layer to the decision-making process. It revolves around the crucial decision of when to cease exploring new options — be it for the perfect house, a romantic partner, or a restaurant — and when to leverage the value of a good find. In areas like investing or dining, once a beneficial option is identified, it makes sense to exploit this advantage, reaping repeated benefits from a well-chosen investment or enjoying a favorite eatery multiple times. This strategy balances the thrill of discovery with the comfort and reliability of known, rewarding choices. The concept of "search versus exploitation" is a critical principle in both computer science and everyday decision-making. It involves a trade-off between exploring new possibilities (search) and making the most of known resources (exploitation). It also applies to your career, when deciding whether to stay in a current job (exploitation) or to seek a new opportunity (search).

Here are some inspiring examples of the search versus exploitation concept:

- Google's Algorithm Updates: Google continually balances between refining its existing search algorithms (exploitation) and experimenting with new ones to improve search results (search).

- Netflix's Recommendation Engine: Netflix's recommendation system is a blend of exploiting known user preferences to suggest movies and exploring new genres or titles that the user might like.

- Career Paths: A professional might choose to explore new job opportunities or industries (search) or could decide to exploit their current position by climbing the corporate ladder within their existing company.

The search vs. exploit compromise can be perfectly illustrated through the restaurant analogy. Imagine you have a favorite restaurant you frequent often. This is 'exploitation' - you know what to expect and enjoy the consistency. However, there's also the allure of 'searching' - trying new restaurants. While there's a risk of disappointment, there's also the chance of discovering a new favorite. This dilemma isn't limited to dining out. It applies to many life choices, such as choosing movies or books. Do you rewatch your favorite film, or try a new one? Similarly, in shopping, do you buy your usual brand, or experiment with a new one? This balance is pivotal in decision-making, helping to navigate the tension between the comfort of the familiar and the excitement of the new.

There are several heuristics that can help in deciding when to transition from search to exploitation:

- Satisficing: This involves setting a threshold for what's acceptable. Once an option meets or exceeds this threshold, you shift from searching to exploiting. For example, in house hunting, you might decide to buy the next house that meets all your essential criteria, rather than searching for a 'perfect' home.

- Cost-Benefit Analysis: Weigh the costs of continued searching (time, effort, missed opportunities) against the potential benefits of finding a better option. For instance, in investing, if the cost and effort of finding a marginally better stock outweigh the potential gains, it's time to exploit the current best option.

- The 37% Rule: In line with optimal stopping theory, this rule suggests exploring options without commitment for the first 37% of your search time or options, and then choosing the next option that's better than what you've seen. This can be applied to situations like job hunting or dating.

These heuristics offer practical frameworks to guide the transition from exploration to exploitation, optimizing decision-making in various scenarios, and balancing the potential benefits of waiting with the risks of losing an opportunity.

For more sophisticated decision-making strategies, techniques like Monte Carlo simulations and Markov Processes offer advanced approaches. Monte Carlo simulations use randomness to simulate a range of possible outcomes, providing a broad perspective on potential scenarios. This is especially useful in complex environments with many variables. Markov Processes, on the other hand, focus on the current state to predict future states, making them ideal for sequential decision-making processes. These methods enhance decision-making by providing a more nuanced understanding of the potential outcomes and their probabilities, allowing for more informed and optimized decisions.

We have already talked about using the power of mathematics and the tools provided by the science behind optimal stopping principles. There are other factors that will influence whether we make a good decision or not, some of them are psychological biases, and there is also how creative we can be in coming with alternative solutions that might not have been obvious at first. In their book "Decisive", Dan and Chip Heath presents an excellent decision making framework that nicely complements the tools we have already discussed.

They call this framework WRAP, based on the four core ideas:

- Widen Your Options: This involves exploring a broad range of choices rather than getting stuck in a narrow mindset. It's about considering multiple possibilities before making a decision.

- Reality-Test Your Assumptions: Testing assumptions against real-world evidence prevents decision-making biases. It involves seeking diverse opinions and verifying facts.

- Attain Distance Before Deciding: Gaining perspective by stepping back from a decision helps to see the bigger picture and reduces emotional bias.

- Prepare to be Wrong: Acknowledging the possibility of error allows for contingency planning and flexibility in decision-making.

It is also importat to determine whether a decision has to be made quickly, or if you can afford to wait. For example, in investing you can sometimes afford to wait a long time before deciding to invest while keeping your money earning some interest. Buffett makes the analogy to a 'no strikes' game, where he can just wait for the perfect pitch before he decides to take a swing. Still, if you take too many years to decide, even if you make a great investment you will have some "cathing up" to do. Some additional strategies that can help with decision include setting a deadline in decisions with a time constraint, or a specific number of options to review. This prevents endless searching and promotes a more decisive approach. After a thorough analysis, if an option feels right, trust your instincts. Often, your subconscious synthesizes information more holistically than you might realize. Finally, prepare to miss out and accept that the nature of probability means you might not always make the 'best' choice, and be comfortable with good enough decisions.

These strategies can be applied to a range of personal and financial decisions, from investing and purchasing to more personal choices, helping to navigate the complexity of options with a balanced approach. If a decision appears to complex, sometimes it helps to beak it down into a number of smaller decision or sub-problems that are easier to evaluate. For example, when building a portfolio you can fist decide how much to allocate to each asset class, and then you can make specific decisions regarding each class of investments.

Take Aways

The science of optimal stopping is a fascinating area of study that intersects with fields such as statistics, mathematics, and computer science. It seeks to determine the best time to take a specific action based on balancing costs and benefits.

When investing, the principle of acting with decisiveness under the right circumstances is crucial. Legendary investors Warren Buffett and Charlie Munger have long advocated for the importance of seizing rare opportunities with conviction. This approach can be likened to having a limited number of trades in a lifetime, say 20, which forces a more meticulous and deliberate evaluation process. Warren Buffett has famously said that "...when it rains gold, put out the bucket, not the thimble". Applying this to broader decision-making, it suggests that while patience and careful analysis are important, there comes a point when one must act decisively. Whether it's in investments, career choices, or personal decisions, the key is to recognize these moments and have the courage to act with conviction.

Often, decisions must be made with incomplete information. While this adds complexity, the outlined strategies provide guidance. While optimal stopping strategies and the WRAP framework have their limitations, especially in real-world scenarios, they offer valuable approaches to tackle complex decisions, enhancing the likelihood of favorable outcomes.

Chapter 11 - The Path to Financial Escape Velocity

"The journey of a thousand miles begins with a single step." – Lao Tzu

Practical Steps to Achieve Financial Independence

There are a few practical steps to get your rocket accelerating towards financial escape velocity. The first is to spend less than you earn, so that you can start saving. There are two ways you can go about achieving this goal, one is simply to spend less, but the other that is considered less often is to earn more. You can find ways to increase your earnings in a number of ways, which could include asking for a raise. If you have good arguments and make the request in a polite and strategic manner, there is a decent chance your employer might agree to it. Then there are more powerful ways to increase your earnings, we already talked about the number of ways you could create passive income streams and micro-businesses.

The second step is to invest shrewdly, but in a smart way, and remain patient during the inevitable ups and downs of the market and the economy. Charlie T. Munger used to say that "if you want to get rich, you'll need a few decent ideas where you really know what you're doing. Then you've got to have the courage to stick with them and take the ups and downs. Not very complicated, and it's very old-fashioned." Prioritize investments with strong competitive moats, whether it's real estate, stocks, or bonds, you want your investments to be resilient. Munger told Buffett, "Forget what you know about buying fair businesses at wonderful prices; instead, buy wonderful businesses at fair prices." If you have high-cost debt, also prioritize paying it off.

The third step is to keep repeating steps one and two until you reach financial escape velocity! Your savings and investments, including your passive income streams, might start small in the beginning. Do not let this discourage you, as long as you keep accelerating you will eventually reach financial escape velocity. Try to keep investments for the long-term, unless you see their competitive moat deteriorate. As Munger used to say, "the big money is not in the buying and the selling, but in the waiting".

Embrace the Magic of Compounding

"Compound interest is the eighth wonder of the world," a quote often attributed to Einstein, illustrates the profound impact of compounding. Although its attribution to Einstein is debated (Aristotle humorously might've said, 'Never trust citations on the internet!'), the idea remains potent. As Munger said, "You don't have to have perfect wisdom to get very rich. Just a bit better than average over a long period of time."

Charlie Munger emphasized the first rule of compounding: never interrupt it unnecessarily. This principle is echoed in Warren Buffett's success, with over 90% of his wealth accumulated after the age of 65. Conversely, compounding can work against you, especially in debt. Once you get into debt it's difficult to get out, especially with high interest credit card debt. Thus, understanding and respecting the power of compounding is crucial in both wealth creation and management.

You can visualize the effect of compounding by imagining a small snowball at the top of a snowy hill. As it rolls down, it gathers more snow, gradually increasing in size. The larger it gets, the more snow it picks up, accelerating its growth exponentially. The cumulative effect of compounding has the potential to transform small beginnings into substantial results over time.

Compounding isn't just a financial concept; it significantly impacts personal growth areas like learning and skill development. Just like small, consistent investments grow over time due to compound interest, regular, incremental learning and skill-building can lead to substantial improvements. For instance, reading a little every day not only expands knowledge gradually but, over time, transforms into a vast repository of understanding and insight. Similarly, practicing a skill regularly, even in small amounts, leads to mastery through the compounding effect of consistent effort. This principle of small, consistent improvements resulting in dramatic changes is a powerful tool in personal development, emphasizing the long-term benefits of persistence and regularity.

Flexibility, Adaptability, and Resourcefulness

The engineering principle of redundancy, involving backup systems for added safety and reliability, is crucial in maintaining financial escape velocity. Just as engineers design systems with backups to ensure functionality during failures, financially independent individuals should create safety nets. This can mean having an emergency fund, diverse income streams, or investments across various asset classes. Such financial redundancy ensures stability even in economic downturns, allowing for flexibility and adaptability. It's about being resourceful, not just in accumulating wealth, but in safeguarding it against unforeseen circumstances, thus securing financial independence in the long term.

Similarly, avoiding Single Points of Failure (SPOFs) is vital in maintaining financial stability. Similar to a family business being the sole income source, other potential SPOFs include relying on a single investment or market. Diversification is key—spreading investments across different sectors, having multiple income streams, and maintaining a well-rounded skill set for employability. Avoiding Single Points of Failure (SPOFs) extends beyond income sources to encompass various aspects of financial planning. Consider the catastrophic impact of an expensive illness without adequate medical coverage, or the repercussions of entrusting all investments to a single broker who might fail. These scenarios underscore the need for a comprehensive approach to risk management. Having health insurance, diversifying brokers and investment platforms, and maintaining a well-rounded portfolio are crucial steps in mitigating such risks. These strategies ensure that financial stability is not jeopardized by a single, unforeseen event, preserving the hard-earned financial escape velocity.

A closely related idea is found in "black swan" events, or long-tail risks. Distinguished Professor Nassim Taleb has popularize this concept, and has been warning about the consequences of ignoring low-probability and high impact risks. These are rare, unforeseeable events with potentially severe consequences. For instance, living or investing heavily in a country with a small risk of war, or selling derivatives for small premiums with potential for huge losses, as insurance giant AIG experienced. Nassim Taleb's quote, "If we visibly incur tiny risk of ruin, but have frequent exposure, it will go to probability one over time," highlights the importance of recognizing and mitigating these low-probability but high-impact risks, especially if they are recurrent.

Adaptability in seizing opportunities is a key component of financial resilience. The adage "Opportunity comes to the prepared mind" encapsulates this idea. Being adaptable means being ready to pivot when unexpected opportunities arise. For instance, Warren Buffett's investment in Apple in 2016, a departure from his typical investment style, showcased adaptability and readiness to seize opportunities outside his traditional approach. Similarly, the rapid shift many businesses made to online platforms during the COVID-19 pandemic is another example of adaptability in action. These instances highlight the importance of staying prepared, flexible, and open to new possibilities for growth and success.

Make sure you are comfortable with uncertainty, and do not take risks that keep you from sleeping well at night. And when markets decline, be ready to take the long-term view and see them as an opportunity to invest at great prices, instead of seeing it as a loss. Remember what Munger used to say in this regard, "If you're not willing to react with equanimity to a market price decline of 50% two or three times a century, you're not fit to be a common shareholder and you deserve the mediocre result you're going to get."

While adaptability is key, it's equally important to avoid over-concentration in a single investment, particularly if it's declining in value. This could indicate underlying issues with the company or sector. Over-concentration increases risk and vulnerability to market fluctuations. Charlie Munger's warning highlights this danger: "Failure to handle psychological denial is a common way for people to go broke: You have made an enormous commitment to something. You have poured effort and money in. And the more you put in, the more that the whole consistency principle makes you think, 'Now it has to work. If I put in just a little more, then it will work.'" This serves as a caution against letting emotional investment and sunk costs drive financial decisions, emphasizing the importance of a balanced, well-reasoned investment strategy.

Finally, we should talk about leverage, or the use of borrowed money to amplify investment returns. While it can significantly increase potential gains, it also magnifies losses. Over-leveraging is a common path to financial ruin, as it can quickly escalate debts beyond manageable levels, especially during market downturns. A notable example of the dangers of leverage is the collapse of Long-Term Capital Management (LTCM). Despite having Nobel Prize-winning economists and renowned financial experts as part of the company, LTCM faced catastrophic failure due to its high leverage strategy. In 1998, the fund's over-reliance on leverage led to its downfall when unforeseen market conditions occurred. This highlights the risks of even the most sophisticated strategies when they are heavily leveraged. Using leverage to buy a house by getting a mortgage can be reasonable, using it to boost the performance of a stock portfolio is almost always a bad idea.

Common Obstacles and How to Overcome Them

Embarking on the journey to financial independence is rarely straightforward. Along the way, individuals inevitably encounter various obstacles. These challenges, ranging from economic fluctuations to personal biases, can significantly impede progress. Recognizing and understanding these hurdles is crucial for navigating the path to financial stability and growth effectively. The following expanded points delve into common obstacles and offer insights on how to overcome them, ensuring a more resilient and strategic approach to achieving and maintaining financial escape velocity.

- Inflation and Unexpected Costs: Inflation can erode purchasing power, while unexpected costs like medical emergencies can derail financial plans. Building a diversified investment portfolio that includes real assets like real estate and infrastructure can hedge against inflation, and maintaining an emergency fund provides a safety net. Make sure to focus on real returns, which for fixed income can mean sometimes considering inflation-protected securities.

- Social Pressures: Requests for loans from friends and relatives can be challenging. It's important to balance generosity with financial prudence. Remember, not all loans are recoverable, and it's okay to say no to protect your financial well-being. In some case a family or friend will really need a loan for an emergency, but in cases where they are asking for money to buy a house or start a business be more careful. Remember Munger's wise words: "The first chance you have to avoid a loss from a foolish loan is by refusing to make it. There is no second chance."

- Client Relationships: The quality of your clients can impact your business success and personal satisfaction. Choosing clients that align with your values can lead to more fulfilling and sustainable business relationships. If possible, choose clients as you would friends, and don't sell anything you wouldn't buy yourself.

- Integrity in Work and Investments: Align your work and investments with your principles. This ensures long-term satisfaction and success, and avoids ethical dilemmas.

- Incentives and Outcomes: Be aware of how incentives influence decisions. Understanding this dynamic helps make more objective decisions in both personal and professional spheres.

- Lifestyle Inflation: As income grows, so can the temptation to increase spending. It's vital to maintain a balance and remember that increasing expenses can slow down or reverse financial progress. Remember Benjamin Franklin wise words, "Beware of little expenses; a small leak will sink a great ship."

- Knowledge and Reality: Acknowledging the limits of your knowledge and accepting reality, even when unpleasant, is crucial for making informed decisions and avoiding costly mistakes. Munger used to say, "Knowing what you don't know is more useful than being brilliant."

- Seeking Advice: Exercise caution with professional advice, especially if it disproportionately benefits the advisor. Seeking second opinions and independent research can be beneficial.

- Behavioral Biases: Understanding and acknowledging personal biases in decision-making can help avoid irrational financial decisions. This awareness is key in maintaining a clear perspective.

- Market Valuations and Consumption: Adjust your spending and investment strategies based on market conditions. This strategic approach can optimize financial growth and stability. As Buffett advises, "Be greedy when others are fearful, and fearful when others are greedy."

Each of these points underscores the multifaceted nature of financial independence, encompassing not just investment strategies but also personal behavior, decision-making, and risk management. If you increase your lifestyle, it is like increasing the force of gravity, and you might return to being below escape velocity.

Case Studies and Real-World Examples

There are many real world examples of people that have achieved financial escape velocity in a variety of ways, at different ages, and with different approaches. Some had relatively low salaries, so they focused on finding a way to minimize expenses so that even if their investment or passive income is not massive, it is enough to sustain them. Others started with side hustles or micro-businesses, that blew up beyond their expectations.

They vary as to how relatable they can be, as some started with some clear advantages, whie others are truly self-made successes. An interesting YouTube channel that shares these types of stories is CNBC Make It. For example, there is the story of an ex-journalist making around $21,000 per year, then quit to become a freelance writer, and finally leveraged her experience to create a successful business.[11] Another interesting story is that of a photographer that turned a side hustle into a $134,000 per year business.[12] What is interesting in both of these examples is that they started very small, and required patience for them to really take off. There are many other well-known examples in the Financial Independence Retire Early (FIRE) community, some of the better known ones include:

- Peter Adeney, better known as Mr. Money Mustache, retired at the young age of 30 through a combination of extreme saving and smart investing. His journey to financial independence began with a lifestyle of remarkable frugality. While working in the tech industry, Peter and his wife managed to save a significant portion of their income. This was not achieved through extreme measures, but rather through a series of well-considered lifestyle choices that prioritized saving and investing over immediate consumption. The lessons from Mr. Money Mustache's story are profound. He advocates for a lifestyle that challenges conventional consumerism, emphasizing minimalism and sustainability. His approach demonstrates that financial freedom isn't about earning a high income, but about how much you save and how effectively you invest those savings. His blog, which details his journey and philosophy, has inspired a movement towards responsible spending and the pursuit of financial independence.

- Kristy Shen and Bryce Leung's journey to financial independence is a story of strategic planning and disciplined saving. Working as computer engineers, they saved diligently and invested in a diversified portfolio. Their approach was methodical, focusing on increasing their savings rate, living below their means, and investing in low-cost index funds. The couple's philosophy of "FIRE" underscores the power of saving and investing to achieve early retirement. They encourage others to adopt a lifestyle that balances frugality with enjoyment, emphasizing that financial independence is not about deprivation but about making intelligent financial choices. Their story is an inspiration for those looking to escape the traditional work-until-retirement model, showing that with the right approach, early retirement is within reach.

---

11 https://www.youtube.com/watch?v=odN3ON4ZVOE
12 https://www.youtube.com/watch?v=m56-QeTP5cg

Take Aways

We have a passion for keeping things simple. Mistakes will be made, but make sure you have a resilient plan that can deal with mistakes, as well as unexpected obstacles. It is very hard to predict the future, so you have to have some diversification, and ideally multiple sources of passive income. It is important to avoid situations with a massive downside and a small upside (like skipping on healthcare coverage), as well as to put leverage on risky or volatile investments. The path to financial freedom is as much about avoiding pitfalls as it is about seizing opportunities. It requires a balance of knowledge, caution, and the willingness to continuously learn and adapt. The road is often paved with challenges and learning opportunities. Small missteps, seemingly insignificant at first, can cumulatively lead to significant problems. It's essential to recognize our limitations, staying within our circle of competence, and commit to lifelong learning, for these are the pillars of long-term success.

Benjamin Graham famously said, "In the short run, the market is a voting machine but in the long run, it is a weighing machine." This quote underlines the importance of assessing the true long-term value of investments, rather than getting swayed by the market's short-term fluctuations. It's a reminder that patience and a focus on fundamental values are key in the financial world. When evaluating a company, a comprehensive assessment of its management and competitive advantage is crucial. This means looking beyond conventional financial metrics to understand factors like management's ability, trustworthiness, and their orientation towards owners. How societal trends and competitive forces might affect the company also plays a significant role in this assessment.

Finally, walk slowly if you are in a hurry, as doing things with patience and care can avoid mistakes and help you reach your goals faster. When it comes to reaching financial scape velocity, the turtle often beats the hare. So be patient, measure twice and cut once, and enjoy the journey as much as the destination!

Chapter 12 - Reusable Rockets

"The real measure of your wealth is how much you'd be worth if you lost all your money." – Anonymous

When it comes to philanthropy, the effectiveness of your donation is as crucial as the act of giving itself. To maximize the impact, it's essential to research and understand the organizations you plan to support. This means delving into their impact metrics, assessing how they utilize funds, and ensuring their goals align with your personal values. Targeted giving, where you focus your resources on specific causes or areas where you feel most passionate, can significantly increase the effectiveness of your contributions. This approach not only ensures that your donations are meaningful but also aligns your philanthropic efforts with your broader life goals.

Philanthropy, much like investing, can have a compounding effect. Initiatives like The Giving Pledge or the donation of the Patagonia company exemplify how large-scale philanthropic commitments can inspire others and create a ripple effect of generosity. These acts of giving demonstrate the power of philanthropy to effect long-term, positive change. Such examples serve as beacons, showing how impactful giving can be when done thoughtfully and strategically. They also illustrate the importance of legacy in philanthropy – how a single act of generosity can continue to impact lives and communities for generations.

The concept of 'paying it forward' is integral to creating a sustainable and supportive community. It's about helping the next generation and those less privileged, providing them with opportunities that might not have been available otherwise. This approach is about building a cycle of support, where today's beneficiaries become tomorrow's benefactors. Such nitiatives often focus on critical areas like education and healthcare, laying the foundation for a stronger, more resilient society. By investing in the future of others, we not only enrich their lives but also contribute to the well-being of the broader community.

In a world of unequal opportunities, philanthropy can be a powerful tool for leveling the playing field. Focusing on individuals and communities that have been less privileged is crucial. Philanthropic efforts in education, healthcare, and community development can have transformative effects on the lives of individuals, opening doors that were previously closed. The stories of success emerging from such initiatives are a testament to the power of thoughtful giving. They underscore the potential of philanthropy to change trajectories, empowering individuals to break cycles of poverty and disadvantage.

One of the most pressing global challenges is climate change. Philanthropic responses have ranged from funding renewable energy projects to supporting environmental conservation efforts. For instance, the Bezos Earth Fund, launched by Jeff Bezos, pledged $10 billion to address climate change. This fund aims to support scientists, activists, NGOs, and others working to protect the natural world and emphasize the importance of collective action in combating climate change.

Philanthropic efforts have also been pivotal in addressing global health crises, such as the COVID-19 pandemic. The Gates Foundation has been at the forefront, committing substantial resources to vaccine development, treatment research, and healthcare system support in various countries. This kind of targeted philanthropy not only addresses immediate needs but also helps build infrastructure for future health challenges.

Education is another area where philanthropy can make a substantial global impact. Organizations like the Malala Fund, co-founded by Nobel laureate Malala Yousafzai, focus on advocating for and investing in education for girls worldwide. By supporting the right to education, these philanthropic efforts aim to empower young women and contribute to broader societal change.

Efforts to combat global poverty have seen significant philanthropic involvement. For example, GiveDirectly is an innovative approach that provides direct cash transfers to people living in extreme poverty. This method has shown significant positive impacts on recipients' lives, challenging traditional models of aid and assistance. Another good example is Kiva.org which lets people lend money to individuals in less developed countries, who would otherwise not have access to a loan or credit at a reasonable rate.

Education is a fundamental driver of personal and societal growth, and philanthropic contributions have significantly shaped this sector. Take, for instance, the story of the Khan Academy. Started by Salman Khan, a hedge fund analyst, it began as a series of online tutorials for his cousins. The potential of these tutorials was recognized by Ann Doerr, wife of venture capitalist John Doerr, who provided the first major donation. This philanthropic act was a catalyst, transforming Khan Academy into a global educational platform, offering free high-quality education to millions.

Philanthropic funding in research has led to groundbreaking discoveries and innovations. The Howard Hughes Medical Institute, one of the largest private funding organizations for biological and medical research in the United States, has played a crucial role in advancing our understanding of health and disease. The Institute supports individual scientists and initiatives, emphasizing the importance of long-term, flexible funding for high-risk, high-reward research.

Innovation in public education is another area where philanthropy has made a mark. Projects like the XQ: The Super School Project, funded by Laurene Powell Jobs' Emerson Collective, are reimagining high school education in America. By providing grants and support, this project encourages schools to develop innovative models that better prepare students for the challenges of the 21st century.

The integration of technology in philanthropy has revolutionized the way we approach charitable giving and social impact. Data analytics is playing a crucial role in understanding the needs and measuring the impact of philanthropic efforts. Organizations like DataKind partner with nonprofits to use data science in enhancing their impact. By analyzing data, charities can optimize their resources, understand the effectiveness of their programs, and make informed decisions about future initiatives.

Artificial intelligence (AI) is aiding philanthropy in addressing complex global challenges. AI algorithms can predict trends, identify areas in need of aid, and optimize resource allocation. For example, AI has been used in analyzing climate patterns to predict and mitigate the effects of natural disasters, helping humanitarian organizations to prepare and respond more effectively.

Take Aways

Once you have accomplished financial independence, you can focus on volunteering and philanthropy, in order to create a more balanced, equitable world. One of the key takeaways is the importance of 'paying it forward.' This concept underscores the idea that not everyone receives equal opportunities in life, and those who have succeeded have a responsibility to help others. This assistance can significantly level the playing field, especially for those who face systemic barriers.

Moreover, for the affluent, the diminishing utility of wealth for personal gain can be transformed into a tool for widespread societal benefit. The concept that additional spending brings little joy when one is already wealthy highlights the opportunity to optimize the 'utility' of wealth by directing it towards those in need. In this way, philanthropy becomes a means of not just giving back but also of deriving meaningful satisfaction from seeing wealth create positive change.

Additionally, philanthropy, when executed effectively, has a compounding effect. By investing in education, for instance, you could be supporting the journey of a future doctor who might discover a cure for a disease. Such investments in human potential multiply their impact over time and across communities, illustrating the far-reaching consequences of thoughtful giving.

Ultimately, the true essence of giving back lies in the understanding that our collective progress hinges on the individual successes of each member of our society. By helping others find and follow their passions, we're not just investing in their futures; we're fostering a more vibrant, diverse, and innovative world. Philanthropy, at its core, is about more than just financial assistance; it's an investment in human potential. Every individual possesses unique talents and passions, often lying dormant or undiscovered due to lack of resources or opportunities. When we, as benefactors, step in to bridge these gaps, we do more than provide temporary relief. We unlock doors to new possibilities, allowing individuals to explore and excel in fields they are truly passionate about.

In the spirit of our cosmic journey, here's a lighthearted nudge to those who've reached their financial stratosphere: "Now that you've enjoyed the view from space, don't forget to send your rocket back down to Earth!" We're all part of this grand mission, and each returned rocket is a beacon of hope, propelling another dreamer into their orbit of success. So, let's keep the cycle going - one rocket at a time!

Chapter 13 – Conclusion

"I skate to where the puck is going to be, not where it has been." -Wayne Gretzky

When making significant personal, financial, or business decisions, such as buying a house or investing in a market, it's crucial to consider not just the present state of things but also their potential future trajectory. This approach, often termed "forward-thinking," involves evaluating the long-term implications and future trends that might influence the current choice.

For instance, in purchasing a house, it's wise to consider the future of the neighborhood. Factors like planned infrastructure, community development, or zoning changes can significantly impact the property's value and livability over time. Similarly, for a house near the beach, the implications of climate change, such as rising sea levels or increased storm frequency, become vital considerations. This forward-looking approach ensures that decisions made today remain beneficial in the long run.

In financial and business contexts, this principle is equally important. Forward-thinking in these areas involves anticipating market trends, technological advancements, and changes in consumer behavior. A business, for example, must consider how emerging technologies might disrupt its industry or how shifts in societal values could affect demand for its products.

However, it's crucial to balance forward-thinking with a healthy skepticism of hype and trends. The saying "what the wise man does in the beginning, the fool does in the end" warns against jumping on bandwagons without critical analysis. Many fads, bubbles, and seemingly promising trends can lead to poor decisions if not carefully scrutinized. For example, during a market bubble, assets may become highly overvalued as investors follow the hype without considering the underlying value or sustainability of the investment. Similarly, in business, chasing the latest trend without a solid understanding of its implications can lead to misallocated resources and strategic missteps.

Thus, while it's wise to look towards the future and anticipate changes, it's equally important to differentiate between enduring trends and fleeting fads. This balance ensures that decisions are both forward-looking and grounded in reality, avoiding the pitfalls of short-term thinking and unfounded speculation.

Future Outlook

One significant trend is the changing landscape of social security and pensions. Many countries are facing the challenge of aging populations, putting pressure on public budgets. This could lead to reduced benefits, higher retirement ages, or even the elimination of certain pension schemes. As a result, individuals may need to place a greater emphasis on personal savings and private pension plans to secure their financial future.

Arguably, one of the most transformative trends is the rise of AI and automation. As these technologies advance, they're expected to significantly reduce the need for labor in various sectors. This shift could lead to job displacement but might also create new opportunities in tech-driven fields. For individuals, this means that continuous learning and adaptability will be key to maintaining employability and financial stability. It also suggests a potential shift in investment strategies, favoring sectors that are at the forefront of technological innovation. The introduction of concepts like Universal Basic Income (UBI) could also play a role. If implemented, UBI could provide a basic level of financial security for all citizens, potentially reducing the need for personal savings. However, its impact on the economy, tax structures, and personal incentive to work remains a topic of debate.

Each of these trends presents both challenges and opportunities for achieving financial independence. Navigating them successfully will require a combination of adaptability, informed decision-making, and proactive financial planning. As the landscape evolves, staying informed and flexible will be crucial for anyone looking to secure their financial future amidst these dynamic changes.

Adaptability in the financial world is not just beneficial; it's essential. The most successful financial strategies are those that evolve. Commit to continuous learning, be open to new ideas, and be ready to adjust your strategies in response to the changing financial environment.

You are now equipped with the knowledge to navigate the path to financial independence. Take these principles and apply them with determination and patience. Set your goals, stay disciplined, and remember, the journey to financial freedom is as rewarding as the destination. Let your journey be driven by knowledge, shaped by wisdom, and enriched by experience.

In the cosmos of wealth, giving back becomes a pivotal force, not just enriching others' lives but also adding depth to our own. Philanthropy and generosity should not be afterthoughts but integral elements of our financial narrative. They reinforce the idea that our wealth's true value lies not in hoarding, but in sharing - in the impact we create and the lives we uplift.

As we conclude, remember that this book is not just a guide but a starting point. Your financial journey is unique, shaped by your aspirations, decisions, and actions. Stay curious, remain vigilant, and always strive to learn more. In the words of Sir Isaac Newton, "What we know is a drop, what we don't know is an ocean." So, keep exploring, keep growing, and let your financial journey be a testament to your resilience and foresight.

In closing, I leave you with a thought to ponder: True wealth isn't measured in currency or assets, but in the richness of the life you lead and the legacy you leave behind. As you achieve your financial escape velocity, consider how your actions, both financial and philanthropic, can echo through time, creating a legacy that transcends material wealth. Remember, the journey is as significant as the destination.